M. Law
95

ISBN 0-941676-36-6

Rice

Chinese Home–Cooking 家常篇

作　　　　者　　林麗華
翻　譯　顧　問　　葛潔輝
出　　版　　者　　純青出版社有限公司
　　　　　　　　台北市松江路125號5樓
　　　　　　　　郵政劃撥12106299
　　　　　　　　電話：(02)5074902 . 5084331
著 作 財 產 權 人　　財團法人味全文化教育基金會
印　　　　刷　　秋雨印刷股份有限公司

Author   Lee Hwa Lin
Translation Consultant   Connie Wolhardt
Publisher   Chin Chin Publishing Co., Ltd.
                              5th fl., 125, Sung Chiang Rd, Taipei, Taiwan, R.O.C.
                              TEL:(02)5074902 . 5084331
Copyright Holder   Wei-Chuan Cultural-Educational Foundation
Printer   Choice Communications Corp
                              Printed in Taiwan R.O.C.
Distributor   Wei-Chuan Publishing
                              1455 Monterey Pass Rd, #110
                              Monterey Park, CA 91754, U.S.A.
                              TEL:(213)2613880 . 2613878
                              FAX:(213)2613299

序

中國人的主食是米，許多人每餐若沒有吃飯，就覺得沒吃飽，可見米飯對中國人的重要性。

米的種類很多，蓬萊米、在來米、圓糯米、長糯米、……等等，由於各種米的特性不同，所以可依「米」的素材，製作出千變萬化不同形式的米食，從米飯、米粉、河粉、蒸肉粉、熟粉、粿條到米苔目……，都是由米延伸出來的產物。

由於米食富於變化且資料收集豐富，因此特將米食食譜分為「傳統篇」與「家常篇」一套兩本。「傳統篇」著重中國古時米食的傳承，盼將一些快失傳的烹調技藝做成忠實的記錄，讓現代炎黃子孫、甚至外國朋友都能品味其中甘美，展現米的魅力。

而這本「家常篇」包含了八十四道精心調味及簡易做法的米食食譜，也提供一些烹飪技巧的圖片，讓初學者更容易瞭解。

現代人行止匆忙，在下班後，能以最短的時間、簡易的材料、迅速的做法，享受一頓色香味俱全的「快餐」堪稱奢求，而這兩本食譜即教導讀者利用不同種類的米，加上一般材料，快速地做出各種簡餐及點心，使入主中饋的職業婦女或單身貴族，不再視做飯為畏途。

Rice is the main staple of Chinese. Many Chinese feel unsatisfied if rice is not served at meals.

There are many different kind of rice : short grain rice, long grain rice, short grain glutinous rice, long grain glutinous rice.....etc.. Due to the differences in their characteristics, rice can be developed into countless variations of recipes, from rice dishes, rice noodles, rice sheets, spiced rice powder for steaming meat, roasted rice flour, rice dough, to Mi Tai Ma; all of these came from the same simple and plain material - rice.

Since the rice foods contain a wide range of variances, this book collected a large selection of different types of rice foods. We divided the recipes into a set of two volumes---"Traditional Cooking" and "Home Cooking". "Traditional Cooking" concentrated more on the rice foods from our ancestry, recording some of the soon disappearing rice recipes and cooking techinques, enable our children and even our foreign friends to appreciate our rice culture and revive the rice glamor of yore.

"Home Cooking" contains 84 tasty and simple-to-make rice recipes. It also includes many pictures of cooking techniques giving the beginners more directions for successful cooking.

With hectic schedules, how to make a good and tasty "fast food dinner", within the shortest time, available materials and simple cooking methods, becomes a real challenge. In these two books, we have detailed the differences of characteristic in each rice, and how to prepare a gourmet rice dinner or snack with rase. Working mothers or singles should no longer consider cooking a fearsome task.

Lee Hwa Lin

目錄 *Contents*

飯的煮法 • *Cooking Methods of Rice*

飯與水的添加計量表 -- Proportion Chart of Rice and Water **7**

特殊材料的製作 • *Preparation Methods of Special Ingredients*

高湯的製作 --Stock **8**
米粉的煮法 --Rice Noodles **8**
鍋粑的製作 --Crisp Rice Cakes **8**
酒釀的製作 ----------------------------------Fermented Wine Rice **9**
熟粉的製作 ----------------------------------Roasted Rice Flour **9**
河粉的製作 ----------------------------------Flat Rice Sheets **9**
五香蒸肉粉的製作 ----------Five-Spice-Flavored Rice Powder **10**
粿粉糰的製作 ------------------------------Rice Flour Dough **10**
粿粉糰之米重與粿粉之重量換算 ----------weight Equivalent **10**
of Rice and Rice Flour for Making Rice Dough
粿粉加水揉成粿粉糰之比例 --- Proportion of Rice Flour and **10**
Water for Making Rice Dough

材料前處理 • *Preparation of Basic Materials*

蔥段的切法 --------------------------Green Onion Sections **11**
香菇的處理 --------------------------Dried Black Mushrooms **11**
腸的清洗方法 ------------------------------------Intestines **11**
蝦仁清洗方法 --Shrimp **12**
筍的處理 ------------------------------------Bamboo Shoots **12**
海參的發法 ----------------------------Dried Sea Cucumber **12**
花枝的處理 --Squids **13**

米粒類 • *Rice*

三鮮鍋粑 ------------Sizzling Rice Cakes with Seafood Sauce **14**
鴛鴦炒飯 ------------------------------------Fried Rice Duet **16**
蛋包飯 --Rice Omelet **18**
翡翠飯 --Green Jade Rice **19**
西班牙飯 --------------------------------------Spanish Paella **20**
海鮮焗飯 ----------------------------Seafood Rice Au Gratin **21**
青椒牛肉燴飯 ------Rice with Green Pepper and Beef Sauce **22**
三鮮燴飯 ------------------------------Rice with Seafood Sauce **24**
家常燴飯 ----------------------------Rice with Home Style Sauce **25**
咖哩燴飯 ----------------------------Rice with Curry Pork Sauce **26**
雞肉羹飯 ----------------------------Chicken Pottage Over Rice **27**
菠蘿炒飯 ----------------------------Pineapple Fried Rice **28**
生炒牛肉飯 ------------------Fried Rice with Beef and Lettuce **30**
青椒牛肉飯 ------------------Green Pepper and Beef Fried Rice **31**
番茄蛋炒飯 --------------------------------Tomato Fried Rice **32**
什錦炒飯 --------------------------------------Mixed Fried Rice **33**
咖哩炒飯 --------------------------------------Curry Fried Rice **34**
海南油雞飯 --------------------------------Hainan Chicken Rice **35**
肉絲炒飯 --------------------Fried Rice with Shredded Pork **36**
火腿蛋炒飯 --------------------Fried Rice with Ham and Eggs **36**

鹹飯糰 --Breakfast Rice Rolls **37**
甜飯糰 --Sweet Rice Rolls **37**
三彩小飯糰----------------------------------Tri-Colored Rice Balls **38**
翡翠小飯糰 --Jade Rice Balls **38**
叉燒小飯糰 ------------------------------Bar-B-Q Pork Rice Balls **39**
香蝦小飯糰 --------------------------------------Shrimp Rice Balls **39**
米飯三明治 --------------------------------------Rice Sandwich **40**
炒飯壽司 --------------------------------------Fried Rice Sushi Rolls **41**
酒釀雞湯 ----------------------------Chicken and Wine Rice Soup **42**
酒釀燒雞 ----------------------------Wine Rice Braised Chicken **42**
珍珠丸子 --Pearl Balls **43**
糯米糕 ----------------------------------Glutinous Rice Cake **43**
涼糕 --Chilled Rice Cake **44**
八寶黑珍珠 ------------------Black Pearls with Candied Fruits **45**
鹹飯 --Salted Rice **46**
油飯 ----------------------------Mixed Rice a la Taiwanese **47**
粉蒸排骨 ----------------------Steamed Ribs with Rice Powder **48**
魯肉飯 --------------------------Rice with Pork Shallot Sauce **49**

粥類 ● *Congee*

粟米粥 --Congee with Corn **50**
絲瓜粥 ------------------------------------Sing Qua Congee **51**
台式鹹粥 ----------------------------Congee a la Taiwanese **52**
香菇竹筍瘦肉粥 ----------Mushrooms and Bamboo Congee **53**
芋頭瘦肉粥 ----------------------------Taro and Pork Congee **54**
雞球粥 --Chicken Congee **54**
南瓜甜粥 ----------------------------Sweet Pumpkin Congee **55**
海鮮粥 --Seafood Congee **55**
鮑魚雞絲粥 ------------------Abalone and Chicken Congee **56**
蟹肉粥 --Crab Congee **57**
桂圓糯米粥 ----------------------------Sweet Logan Congee **58**
綠豆粥 ----------------------------Sweet Green Bean Congee **58**

米漿類 ● *Rice puree*

花生糊 ----------------------------------Peanuts Porridge **59**
核桃酪 --Walnuts Milk **59**
三絲腸粉捲 ----------------------------Pork Rice Sheet Rolls **60**
牛肉粉捲 ----------------------------Beef Rice Sheet Rolls **61**
蝦仁河粉捲 ----------------------------Shrimp Rice Sheet Rolls **62**
干炒牛肉河粉 ------------------------Fried Beef Rice Fettuccini **63**
芋頭糕 --------------------------------------Taro Rice Cake **64**
蘿蔔糕 ----------------------------------Turnip Cake **64**
紅豆糕 ----------------------------------Ruby Rice Cake **65**
發糕 ----------------------------Rice Cake with Soda **65**
蚵碟 --------------------------------Golden Oyster Buns **66**
碗粿 --------------------------------------Pork Wa Guey **67**
甜碗粿 ----------------------------------Sweet Wa Guey **68**
米奶 --Rice Milk **68**

漿糰類 ● *Rice Dough*

芝麻糯米球 ----------------------Sesame Seeds Rice Balls **69**
酒釀湯圓 ----------------------Sweet Wine Rice Dough Balls **69**
鹹湯圓 ----------------------------------Shallot Rice Balls **70**
炸元宵 ----------------------------------Fried Yuan Hsiao **71**

椰絲糯米球 ----------------------------Coconut Rice Dough Balls **72**
軟脆豆沙捲 ----------------------------Crispy Red Bean Rolls **73**
粿粽 --Guey Dumplings **74**
菜包粿 --------------------------------------Tsai Pao Guey **76**
鹹水餃 ----------------------------Fried Pork Dumplings **78**
南瓜糕 ----------------------------Pumpkin Rice Cake **80**
炒寧波年糕 ----------------------------Fried Nin Po Rice Cakes **82**

米粉類 • *Rice Noodles*

三絲炒米苔目 ----------------------------Fried Pork Mi Tai Ma **83**
米粉羹 ----------------------------------Rice Noodles Pottage **84**
擔擔米粉 ----------------------------Dan Dan Rice Noodles **86**
海鮮米粉 ----------------------------Seafood Rice Noodles **88**
酸辣米粉 ----------------------Sour and Spicy Rice Noodles **90**
星洲炒米粉 -------------------Singaporean Fried Rice Noodles **92**
南瓜炒米粉 ----------------------Pumpkin Fried Rice Noodles **93**

重量換算表 • *Measurement Equivalents*

1磅 = 454公克 = 16盎士
1盎士 = 28.4公克
1lb.= 454gm (454g.) = 16oz.
1oz. = 28.4gm (28.4g.)

量器說明 • *Table of Measurements*

1杯 = 236c.c. = 1 cup (1C.)
1大匙 = 1湯匙 = 15c.c. = 1 Tablespoon (1T.)
1小匙 = 1茶匙 = 5c.c. = 1 Teaspoon (1t.)

飯的煮法 • *Cooking Methods of Rice*

1 蓬萊米1杯（２００公克），洗淨瀝乾再加水1杯，放入電鍋中外鍋加水 ¼ 杯煮至電鍋跳起，再續燜五分鐘即為白飯（約４１５公克）。

2 圓糯米1杯（２００公克），洗淨瀝乾再加水 ⅘ 杯，放入電鍋中外鍋加水 ¼ 杯煮至電鍋跳起，再續燜五分鐘即為糯米飯（約３９０公克）。

3 長糯米1杯（１９０公克），洗淨瀝乾再加水 ¾ 杯，放入電鍋中外鍋加水 ¼ 杯煮至電鍋跳起，再續燜五分鐘即為糯米飯（約３６０公克）。另長糯米洗淨後泡水２小時，再瀝乾水分，入蒸鍋中蒸２０分鐘至熟（約３３０公克）是糯米飯另一做法。

■本食譜之白飯是指用蓬萊米所煮成之飯。

1 To cook Japonica Rice (Short Grain Rice): Rinse 1C. (200g. or 7oz.) japonica rice, drain. Add 1C. water and place in a rice cooker, add ¼C. water in the outer pot, then cook until rice cooker shuts off. Continue simmering for 5 minutes extra. Makes 415g. or 14³/₅oz. cooked rice.

2 To cook Short Grain Glutinous Rice: Rinse 1C. (200g. or 7oz.) short grain glutinous rice, drain. Add ⅘C. water and place in a rice cooker, add ¼C. water in the outer pot, and cook until rice cooker shuts off. Continue simmering for 5 minutes extra. Makes 390g. or 13¼oz. cooked glutinous rice.

3 To cook Long Grain Glutinous Rice: Rinse 1C. (190g. or 6²/₃oz.) long grain glutinous rice, drain. Add ¾C. water and place in a rice cooker, add ¼C. water in the outer pot, and cook until rice cooker shuts off. Continue simmering for 5 minutes extra. Makes 360g. or 12 ²/₃oz. cooked glutinous rice. Or: soak long grain glutinous rice in water for 2 hours, drain. Steam for 20 minutes or until cooked (makes 330g. or 11³/₅oz.).

■All cooked rice recipes in this book use cooked short grain rice, unless otherwise indicated.

飯與水的添加計量表 • *Proportion Chart of Rice and Water*

1 若用電子鍋煮飯，則內鍋水分與電鍋煮法相同，但外鍋不需加水。其水分添加計算如下表。

類別	蓬萊米或在來米			圓糯米		長糯米		
米量（公克）	480	300	240	300	200	400	300	480
添加水量（杯）	2 ²/₅	1 ½	1 ⅕	1 ⅕	⅘	1 ³/₅	1 ⅕	1 ⁴/₅

1 If cooking by eletronic rice cooker, no water is needed for outer pot. Water added in the rice is the same as rice cooker. The proportion of rice and water are as following.

Name	Japonica Rice (Short Grain Rice) Indica Rice (Long Grain Rice)			Short Grain Glutinous Rice		Long Grain Glutinous Rice		
Weight of Rice (g.)	480	300	240	300	200	400	300	480
(oz.)	17	10½	8²/₅	10½	70	14	10½	17
Volume of Water (cups)	2²/₅	1½	1⅕	1⅕	⅘	1³/₅	1⅕	1⁴/₅

特殊材料的製作 · *Preparation Methods of Special Ingredients*

高湯的製作 · *Stock*

1 以豬、牛、雞的肉或骨入沸水中川燙。
2 再將肉或骨頭取出洗淨。
3 以另一鍋水燒開後，再入洗淨的肉或骨頭，並加少許蔥、薑、酒慢火熬出來的湯，謂之高湯。

1 Scald pork, beef, chicken or bones in boiling water.
2 Lift out and rinse.
3 Bring clean water to a boil, add meat or bones together with a little green onion, ginger, and cooking wine. Simmer over low heat until the soup is tasty.

 1
 2

 3

米粉的煮法 · *Rice Noodles*

1 米粉的種類有乾的、濕的、粗的、細的等四種。
2 水煮開，入米粉煮軟後隨即撈起，再入鍋炒或煮均可。
3 米粉亦可直接泡冷水或熱水至軟後撈出再入鍋炒或煮均可。

1 There are four kinds of rice noodles:
a. dried   b. fresh   c. thin   d. thick
2 Bring water to a boil, add rice noodles to cook until softened. Remove immediately. May be used for frying or in soup.
3 Instead of boiling, rice noodles may also be soaked in cold or warm water until softened. Drain and use for frying or in soup.

 1
 2

 3

鍋粑的製作 · *Crisp Rice Cakes*

1 圓糯米洗淨，以糯米十分之九的水分略為浸泡，入電鍋煮熟後，打鬆吹涼再平鋪於烤盤上。
2 將米飯壓緊，入烤箱中，以７０℃烤至米粒全乾即可取出切塊，是為鍋粑。

1 Rinse short grain glutinous rice, soak in water (in proportion of ⁹/₁₀ to rice) for a while. Cook in rice cooker until done. Break loose, let cool and spread a even layer on a baking sheet.
2 Pack tight the rice layer, and place in a 70°C (158°F) oven until rice is all dried. Cut into serving pieces for crisp rice cakes.

 1
 2

酒釀的製作 • *Fermented Wine Rice*

1 圓糯米３杯洗淨，加水３杯煮熟後，打鬆吹涼。
2 酒麴１‧５公克，壓碎拌入米飯中。
3 米飯裝入玻璃罐（罐子須擦乾），置於陰涼處使其發酵即為酒釀。

1 Rinse 3C. short grain glutinous rice, add 3C. water and cook until done. Break loose and let cool.
2 Crush 1.5g. fermenting yeast (peka), and mix into the rice.
3 Put into a clean jar (must be wiped dry) and leave it at a cool and dark place to ferment.

熟粉的製作 • *Roasted Rice Flour*

1 熟粉的種類有熟糯米粉及熟在來米粉，其製作方法為米磨成的粉末入鍋小火乾炒１０－１５分鐘至香味出來，且顏色由白色轉為淡黃色即可。

1 There are two kinds of roasted rice flour, one is roasted glutinous rice flour, the other roasted Indica rice flour. The methods are the same: Ground the rice into fine powder, stir fry in a wok over low heat for 10 - 15 minutes until fragrant. The color should turn into a light yellow.

河粉的製作 • *Flat Rice Sheets*

在來米 --------- ２００公克	太白粉 -------------- １½大匙

1 米洗淨泡水２小時後，瀝乾再加２杯水入果汁機中打成米漿，續入太白粉拌勻備用。
2 平盤中塗少許沙拉油，再倒入薄薄一層米漿，入鍋蒸１０分鐘，取出待涼即可。

200g.(7oz.) - Indica rice (long grain rice)	1½T. -------- corn starch

1 Rinse rice and soak in water for 2 hours. Drain and add 2C. water, puree in a blender. Mix well with corn starch.
2 Grease a flat pan with a little salad oil, pour in a thin layer of rice puree. Steam for 10 minutes, remove and allow to cool.

五香蒸肉粉的製作 • *Five-Spice-Flavored Rice Powder*

圓糯米、蓬萊米 ┄┄┄┄┄┄
┄┄┄┄┄┄ 各１５０公克

1 ┌ 五香粉、肉桂粉、花
　　└ 椒粉 ┄┄┄┄ 各½小匙

1 米洗淨瀝乾，入乾鍋內以小火炒至水乾後，再加**1**料一起拌
　炒至米呈焦黃色，取出待涼。
2 將炒好的米粒以拌麵棍碾碎即可。

1　　　　　2

150g.(5⅓oz.)each -----
short grain glutinous
rice, japonica rice (short
grain rice)

1 ┌ •½t.each five spices
　　│ powder, cinnamon
　　│ powder, Szechwan
　　└ pepper powder

1 Rinse rice and drain. Stir fry in a wok over low
heat until dry. Stir in **1** and fry until rice turns into
a burned yellow color. Remove and let cool.
2 Crush rice with a rolling pin into fine powder.

粿粉糰的製作 • *Rice Flour Dough*

1 圓糯米６００公克洗淨，加水浸泡３小時後，瀝乾水分，分兩次將米加水用果汁機或磨米機製成米漿，裝入
棉布袋中。
2 布袋口紮緊，用重物壓乾或用脫水機脫去水分。
3 脫水到剩約８００公克之粉糰即為粿粉糰。
4 粿粉糰之另一做法為市售糯米粉或在來米粉（兩者亦可稱粿粉）加水揉成之糰。

粿粉糰之米重與粿粉之重量換算	
米重	粿粉重量
６００公克	４８０公克
９００公克	７２０公克

粿粉加水揉成粿粉糰之比例		
粿粉重量	加水量	粿粉糰重量
４８０公克	1⅓杯	８００公克
７２０公克	2杯	１２００公克

1 Rinse 600g. (1⅓lb.) short grain glutinous rice, soak in water for 3 hours, drain. Divide into 2
portions, add water and puree in a blender. Puree both and place into a cloth bag.
2 Tie the bag opening tightly. Press the bag with a heavy weight or drainer to drain off all liquid.
3 Drain until the dough weighs about 800g. (1¾lb.). This is the rice flour dough ready for use.
4 Or: purchase ready-made glutinous rice flour or Indica rice flour (long grain rice flour) in the market
(both are called rice flour), add water and knead into dough.

Weight Equivalent of Rice and Rice Flour for Making Rice Dough	
Weight of Rice	Weight of Rice Flour
600g. or 1⅓lb.	480g. or 17oz.
900g. or 2lb.	720g. or 1½oz.

Proportion of Rice Flour and Water for Making Rice Dough		
Weight of Rice Flour	Volume of Water	Weight of Rice Dough
480g. or 17oz.	1⅓C.	800g. or 1¾lb.
720g. or 1½lb.	2C.	1200g. or 2⅗lb.

材料前處理 · *Preparation of Basic Materials*

蔥段的切法 · *Green Onion Sections*

1 蔥洗淨。
2 去頭、尾部分。
3 切成3公分長段。

1 Wash green onions.
2 Trim off the tops and roots.
3 Cut into 3 cm (1⅕") long sections.

2

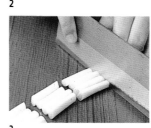

3

香菇的處理 · *Dried Black Mushrooms*

1 香菇用熱水泡軟再洗淨。
2 去蒂頭即可。

1 Soften the mushrooms in warm water, rinse.
2 Discard the stems.

1　2

腸的清洗方法 · *Intestines*

1 大腸、小腸均先將腸壁上之肥油剝掉後清洗乾淨。
2 翻內面，加麵粉、鹽搓洗幾次後，加水沖洗乾淨。
3 入開水中川燙後，取出再洗淨即可。
■ 本食譜之大腸、小腸生重是指洗淨而未川燙之重，熟重是指川燙後再煮至熟爛之重，一般大腸之熟重約只有生重之五分之一，小腸之熟重約只有生重之三分之一。

1 For both large pork intestines and small pork intestines,scrape off outer layer of fat and rinse.
2 Rub flour and salt mixture into inner and outer intestines a few times, rinse.
3 Parboil in boiling water, lift out and wash again.
■ Raw weight in this cook book means washed but not yet parboiled. Cooked weight means the net weight after it has been parboiled and then simmered tender. Generally speaking, large intestine's cooked weight is only ⅕ of raw weight; small intestine's cooked weight is only ⅓ of raw weight.

1　2

3

蝦仁清洗方法 • *Shrimp*

1 蝦用牙籤由背面挑去腸泥（若帶殼，則先去殼）。
2 加太白粉、鹽，輕輕拌洗。
3 用清水洗淨瀝乾，再用布擦乾水分。

1 Devein the shrimp with toothpick (must be shelled first).
2 Clean shrimp by rubbing gently with corn starch and salt.
3 Rinse under water and drain.

1

2

3

筍的處理 • *Bamboo Shoots*

1 新鮮筍中間劃一刀去殼。
2 入水中煮至熟，再取出漂涼即可。若是罐頭筍，有些因製罐關係，會帶有些微酸味，可以先入鍋川燙以去酸味。

1 Cut lengthwise once on the hard outer shell, and peel off all of the outer shell.
2 Boil in water until cooked, drain and let cool.
■ If canned bamboo shoots are used, the taste will be slightly sour due to canning; scald in boiling water to get rid off sour taste before cooking.

1

2

海參的發法 • *Dried Sea Cucumber*

1 乾海參洗淨，泡水一天，隔天換水煮開，煮開後熄火浸泡，待水涼再換水煮開，熄火浸泡，如此一天三次，連續發兩天至軟。
2 由腹部剪開，取出內臟洗淨加水煮開，再發一天即可。
3 若買發好之海參，則剪開肚子取出內臟洗淨即可。

1 Wash the dried sea cucumber, then soak in water for one day. Place sea cucumber into clean water and bring to a boil; turn off the heat and soak until water cools. Change the water again and bring to a boil; turn off the heat and continue soaking until water cools. Repeat the process 3 times a day for 2 days until sea cucumber is softened.
2 Snip open lengthwise and clean out the intestines. Cover with water and bring to a boil. Remove from heat and let it stand for one more day. Then it is ready for cooking.
3 Already soaked sea cucumber can also be bought, then it only needs to be snipped open lengthwise and cleaned out.

1

2

3

花枝的處理・*Squids*

1 花枝去皮、頸。
2 去除內臟，並用水洗淨。
3 花枝肉之內面，每隔0．3公分縱橫切入 ⅓ 深度，使肉身作交叉片狀。
4 將片狀花枝切成4公分寬之條狀。
5 每一條花枝肉再切成4×5公分之片狀。

1 Discard the neck and peel off the skin.
2 Discard the inner gut and wash clean.
3 Score inner surface lengthwise and crosswise every 0.3 cm (¹⁄₁₀") and ⅓ deep into the flesh.
4 Cut into 4 cm (1³⁄₅") wide large strips.
5 Then cut each strip into 4 cm x 5 cm (1³⁄₅" x 2") serving pieces.

1   2

3   4

5

三鮮鍋粑

• *Sizzling Rice Cakes with Seafood Sauce*

三鮮鍋粑 •*Sizzling Rice Cakes with Seafood Sauce*

鍋粑 ----------------- １３０公克
海參、蝦仁、花枝（淨重）---
----------------- 各１００公克
胡蘿蔔 ----------------- ８０公克
豌豆莢 ----------------- ３０公克
香菇 ----------------- ２５公克
蔥段 ----------------- １２段
薑片 ----------------- ４片

1┌ 酒 ----------------- ２大匙
　│ 黑醋 ----------------- １小匙
　│ 鹽 ----------------- ³/₄小匙
　└ 味精 ----------------- ¹/₄小匙

2┌ 水 ----------------- １大匙
　└ 太白粉 ----------------- ２小匙

1 海參、蝦仁、花枝洗淨，海參切片，蝦仁從背部劃開，花枝切花刀片狀，胡蘿蔔切片狀，豌豆莢去老纖維，香菇泡軟去蒂切片備用。

2 鍋熱入油３大匙燒熱，入蔥段、薑片爆香，續入香菇炒香後，再入海參、蝦仁、花枝及胡蘿蔔拌炒均勻，續入水２杯煮開，再加**1**料調味，並以**2**料芶芡備用。

3 另鍋熱入油４杯燒至七分熱（１６０℃），入鍋粑炸至膨起，撈起瀝油，置於盤上，趁熱淋上**2**項材料即可。

130g.(4³/₅oz.) --------------------------------crisp rice cakes
100g.(3¹/₂oz.) each --------sea cucumber, shelled shrimp,
squids (net weight)
80g.(2⁴/₅oz.) ---carrots
30g.(1oz.) -----------------------------------snow pea pods
25g.(⁸/₉oz.) --------------------------dried black mushrooms
12 sections ----------------------------------green onion
4 slices --ginger

1┌ •2T.cooking wine
　│ •1t.brown vinegar
　└ •³/₄t.salt

2┌ •1T.water
　└ •2t.corn starch

1 Wash sea cucumber, shrimp, and squids. Cut sea cucumber and carrots into serving slices. Slit shrimp open on the back. Cut squids into serving pieces. Remove tough fibers of snow pea pods. Soften mushrooms in water, discard the stems, and slice.

2 Heat the wok, add 3T. oil and heat; stir fry green onion sections and ginger slices until fragrant. Add mushrooms to fry until fragrant. Then add sea cucumber, shrimp, squids, and carrots, stir fry and mix well. Add 2C. water and bring to a boil, season with **1**; thicken with **2**.

3 Heat another wok, add 4C. oil and heat to 160°C (320°F); deep fry rice cakes until puffed up, lift out and drain. Place in a plate, pour sauce over the crisp rice cakes and serve hot.

鴛鴦炒飯

•*Fried Rice Duet*

二人份　　**serve　2**

鴛鴦炒飯 • *Fried Rice Duet*

白飯	600公克
蝦仁	115公克
熟青豆仁	80公克
洋火腿丁	30公克
蛋	2個
蔥末	2½大匙
薑末	½大匙

1 鹽、蛋白 各少許

2
鹽	½小匙
味精	¼小匙
胡椒粉	⅛小匙

3
番茄醬	1大匙
糖	½小匙
鹽、味精	各¼小匙

1 蝦仁洗淨，瀝乾水分，入 **1** 料醃約10分鐘，蛋打散備用。

2 鍋熱入油1杯燒至六分熱（140c），入蝦仁炒熟盛起，鍋內留油2大匙燒熱，入蛋液炒成蛋花盛起，續入油½大匙燒熱，入薑末、蔥末各½大匙及洋火腿丁炒香，隨入白飯300公克、**2** 料、蛋花半量、蝦仁40公克及熟青豆仁30公克炒拌均勻即可起鍋。

3 另鍋熱入油½大匙燒熱，炒香蔥末2大匙，隨入白飯300公克及 **3** 料炒勻，最後再加入剩餘之蝦仁、青豆仁、蛋花拌勻即可。

4 將兩種炒飯分別盛放在盤的兩邊，即為鴛鴦炒飯。

600g.(1⅓lb.)	cooked rice
115g.(4oz.)	shelled shrimp
80g.(2⅘oz.)	boiled green peas
30g.(1oz.)	diced ham
2	eggs
2½T.	minced green onion
½T.	minced ginger

1
- •dash of each: salt, egg white

2
- •½t.salt
- •⅛t.pepper

3
- •1T.ketchup
- •½t.sugar
- •¼t.salt

1 Wash shrimp, then drain. Marinate with **1** for 10 minutes. Beat the eggs.

2 Heat the wok, add 1C. oil and heat to 140°C (284°F); stir fry shrimp until cooked, remove. Keep 2T. oil in the wok and heat, stir fry beaten eggs until softly scrambled, remove. Add ½T. oil and heat, stir fry ½T. each minced ginger and minced green onion, and ham until fragrant. Stir in 300g.(10½oz.) rice, **2**, and half of fried eggs, 40g.(1⅖oz.) shrimp, 30g.(1oz.) boiled green peas; stir fry and mix well. Remove.

3 In another wok, add ½T. oil and heat; stir fry 2T. minced green onion until fragrant. Add 300g.(10½ oz.) rice and **3**, mix well. Then add rest of shrimp, green peas, and fried eggs; stir fry and mix well. Remove.

4 Place two fried rice on two sides of a plate.

蛋包飯 • *Rice Omelet*

白飯 ----------------- 4 0 0公克　　蛋 ----------------------- 4 個
雞胸肉、洋蔥 --- 各150公克

1
　鹽、味精 --------- 各¼小匙
　胡椒粉 ------------- ⅛小匙

2
　番茄醬 ------------- 3 大匙
　鹽、糖 ----------- 各½小匙
　味精 ----------------- ¼小匙
　胡椒粉 ------------- ⅛小匙

3
　鹽 ------------------- ¼小匙
　胡椒粉 ------------- ⅛小匙

1 洋蔥切小丁，雞胸肉切小丁入 **1** 料拌醃數分鐘。
2 鍋熱入油2大匙燒熱，將洋蔥丁炒香後，入雞肉同炒，見肉色轉白，再加入白飯及 **2** 料拌炒均勻盛起，分成2份。
3 蛋打散，入 **3** 料拌勻，鍋熱入油1大匙燒熱，將蛋液煎成兩張蛋皮，每張蛋皮煎半熟時（圖1），將炒飯置於蛋皮上（圖2），再包捲起來（圖3）煎至蛋皮全熟即可。

400g.(14oz.) - cooked rice　　4 ----------------------- eggs
150g.(5⅓oz.)each ---------
chicken breast, onion

1
　• ¼t.salt
　• ⅛t.pepper

2
　• 3T.ketchup
　• ½t.each salt, sugar
　• ⅛t.pepper

3
　• ¼t.salt
　• ⅛t.pepper

1 Dice onion. Dice chicken and marinate in **1** for few minutes.
2 Heat the wok, add 2T. oil, stir fry onion until fragrant. Stir in chicken, when color turns white, add rice and **2**, mix well then remove. Divide to two portions.
3 Beat eggs, mix with **3**. Heat the wok, add 1T. oil, make two egg crepes. When each crepe is half done (illus. 1), place fried rice on one half of the egg crepe (illus. 2) and fold over the other half (illus. 3). Fry until egg crepe is golden and serve.

1

2

3

翡翠飯 • *Green Jade Rice*

白飯 ----------------- 6 0 0公克	蔥末 ---------------------- 5 大匙	600g.(1⅓lb.) - cooked rice	5T. -- minced green onion
青江菜 -------------- 2 0 0公克	蒜末 ---------------------- ½大匙	200g.(7oz.) ------ bok choy	½T. ---------- minced garlic
洋火腿 ----------------- 7 5公克	鹽 ------------------------ 1 小匙	75g.(2⅔oz.) ---------- ham	1t. -----------------------salt
蛋 ----------------------------- 2 個		2 ----------------------- eggs	

1 ┌ 鹽 ------------------- ¾小匙
　 └ 味精、胡椒粉 --- 各¼小匙

1 ┌ • ¾t.salt
　 └ • ¼t.pepper

1 青江菜洗淨入鹽1小匙，醃漬2 0分鐘後，洗淨並擠乾水分，再剁碎。

2 火腿切1公分立方塊，蛋打散備用。

3 鍋熱入油1½大匙燒熱，入蛋液炒成蛋花盛起，續入油1½大匙燒熱，入蔥、蒜及火腿爆香，再入白飯及 **1** 料炒勻，最後入蛋花、青江菜末拌勻即可。

1 Wash bok choy and drain, marinate with 1t. salt for 20 minutes. Rinse bok choy and squeeze off liquid, chop finely.

2 Cut ham into 1 cm (⅖") small cubes. Beat the eggs.

3 Heat the wok, add 1½T. oil and heat; stir fry beaten eggs until softly formed, then remove. Add 1 ½T. oil into the wok and heat, stir fry green onion, garlic, and ham until fragrant. Mix in rice and **1** evenly. Then add eggs and bok choy, mix well.

西班牙飯 ·*Spanish Paella*

蓬萊米、蛤蜊 --- 各300公克	花枝（淨重）、劍蝦、洋蔥 ---		
雞胸肉 -------------- 150公克	--------------------- 各100公克		
	青豆仁 ----------------- 60公克		

1
- 番茄糊 ------------- 3 大匙
- 番茄醬 ------------- 1 大匙
- 鹽、味精 --------- 各½小匙
- 披薩香料、迷迭香料 -----
- ------------------- 各¼小匙
- 月桂葉 -------------- 1 葉

2
- 太白粉 ------------- 1 小匙
- 鹽 --------------------- ⅛小匙

1 雞胸肉洗淨切2×2公分薄片，入 **2** 料醃5分鐘。洋蔥切末，米洗淨入¾杯水泡20分鐘，花枝洗淨切花刀備用。

2 鍋熱入油 3 大匙燒熱，爆香洋蔥，續入 **1** 料炒勻，再入½杯水煮開，改小火煮5分鐘，最後將其餘材料入鍋拌勻，再入電鍋內鍋中，外鍋加水 ½ 杯，煮至跳起，再燜10分鐘即可。

300g.(10½oz.) each ------- short grain rice, clams
150g.(5⅓oz.) ------ chicken breast

100g.(3½oz.) each squids (net weight), shrimp, onion
60g.(2¹⁄₁₀oz.) -- green peas

1
- 3T.tomato paste
- 1T.ketchup
- ½t.salt
- ¼t.each pizza seasoning, rosemary
- 1 bay leaf

2
- 1t.corn starch
- ⅛t.salt

1 Wash chicken breast, cut into 2 cm x 2 cm (¾" x ¾") thin slices, and marinate with **2** for 5 minutes. Mince onion; wash rice, soak in ¾C. water for 20 minutes. Wash squids and cut into serving pieces.

2 Heat the wok, add 3T. oil and heat; stir fry onion until fragrant. Add **1** to fry and mix well. Add ½C. water and bring to a boil, simmer over low heat for 5 minutes. Then add the rest of materials, mix well. Place in a rice cooker, add ½C. water in outer pot and boil until rice cooker shuts off. Continue simmering with lid covered for extra 10 minutes.

海鮮焗飯 • *Seafood Rice Au Gratin*

白飯 ----------------- ５００公克	蝦仁 -------------------- ７５公克
花枝（淨重）------ １２０公克	青花菜 ----------------- ７０公克
洋蔥 ----------------- １００公克	蛋 ------------------------- ２個
奶油 ----------------- ８０公克	麵粉 --------------------- ½杯

1
- 水 -------------------- ３杯
- 鹽 -------------------- ¾小匙
- 味精 ----------------- ½小匙
- 黑胡椒粉 ----------- ¼小匙

1 青花菜洗淨去老葉，蛋打散，洋蔥切末，花枝切３×２公分片，蝦仁洗淨備用。

2 鍋熱，入奶油爆香洋蔥，續入蛋液炒熟，再入麵粉炒至微黃，最後加入 **1** 料調勻煮開，即為焗飯醬汁。

3 取一盅（可以入烤箱之材質）入 ⅓ 焗飯醬汁，再入白飯，剩餘醬汁把花枝、蝦仁、青花菜拌勻淋在白飯上，入烤箱上火２００℃、下火２５０℃烤至表面呈金黃（約２０分鐘）即可。

500g.(1¹⁄₁₀lb.) - cooked rice	75g.(2²⁄₃oz.) -------- shelled shrimp
120g.(4¼oz.) ------- squids	70g.(2½oz.) ------- broccoli
100g.(3½oz.) -------- onion	2 ----------------------- eggs
80g.(2⁴⁄₅oz.) ----- butter or margarine	½C. --------------------- flour

1
- •3C.water
- •¾t.salt
- •¼t.pepper

1 Wash broccoli and peel off tough outer fibers. Beat the eggs. Mince onion. Score diagonal crosses on the surface of the squids and cut into serving pieces. Wash shrimp.

2 Heat the wok, add butter or margarine, stir fry onion until fragrant. Add beaten eggs, stir fry until cooked. Then stir in flour and fry until slightly browned. Pour in **1**, mix well and bring to a boil. This is the gratin sauce.

3 Pour ⅓ gratin sauce into a baking casserole, add rice, mix the rest sauce with squids, shrimp, and broccoli, pour over rice. Place the casserole in a pre-heated oven, bake under 200°C (392°F) grill or in 250°C (482°F) oven until golden on top (about 20 minutes).

•*Rice with Green Pepper and Beef Sauce*

四人份　**serve 4**

青椒牛肉燴飯 • *Rice with Green Pepper and Beef Sauce*

白飯 -------------- 1000公克
牛里肌肉 ----------- 300公克
青椒 --------------- 155公克
蔥末 ----------------- 5大匙
薑末、麻油 --------- 各2大匙
紅辣椒 ---------------- 2條

1
- 水、蛋白 -------- 各2大匙
- 醬油、薑酒汁、油 --------
  ------------------- 各1大匙
- 糖 ----------------- 1小匙
- 小蘇打 ----------- 1/2小匙
- 鹽 ----------------- 1/4小匙

2
- 水 ------------------- 3杯
- 醬油、蠔油 ----- 各2大匙
- 糖 ----------------- 2小匙
- 鹽 ----------------- 1小匙
- 胡椒粉 ------------- 1/8小匙

3
- 水 ---------------- 2 1/2大匙
- 太白粉 --------- 1 1/4大匙

1 牛肉逆紋切薄片，入**1**料醃10分鐘。
2 青椒、紅辣椒去籽，均切3×2公分塊狀。
3 鍋熱入油4杯燒熱，入青椒過油隨即撈起，再將牛肉入鍋過油至變色隨即撈起。
4 鍋中留油2大匙，入蔥末、薑末、紅辣椒丁爆香，續入**2**料煮開，以**3**料芶芡，再放入青椒、牛肉炒勻，灑上麻油並拌勻，再淋於白飯上即可。

1000g.(2 1/5oz.) ----------------------- cooked rice
300g.(10 1/2oz.) ------------------------- beef fillet
155g.(5 1/2oz.) ----------------------- green pepper
5T. --------------------------- minced green onion
2T.each ----------------- minced ginger, sesame oil
2 --------------------------------- red chili peppers

1
- 2T.each water, egg white
- 1T.each soy sauce, ginger wine juice, oil
- 1t.sugar
- 1/2t.baking soda
- 1/4t.salt

2
- 3C.water
- 2T.each soy sauce, oyster sauce
- 2t.sugar
- 1t.salt
- 1/8t.pepper

3
- 2 1/2T.water
- 1 1/4T.corn starch

1 Slice beef thin across the grain, marinate in **1** for 10 minutes.
2 Discard seeds in green pepper and red chili peppers, cut both into 3 cm x 2 cm (1 1/5" x 3/4") pieces.
3 Heat the wok, add 4C. oil and heat; dip green pepper in oil, remove immediately. Then fry beef in oil until color changes and remove immediately.
4 Keep 2T. oil in the wok, stir fry minced green onion, minced ginger, and red chili peppers until fragrannt. Add **2** and bring to a boil. Thicken with **3**, stir in green pepper and beef, mix well. Sprinkle on sesame oil and mix. Pour over rice and serve.

三鮮燴飯 • *Rice with Seafood Sauce*

白飯 ------------- 1000公克	蔥段 --------------------- 12段	1000g.(2⅕lb.) cooked rice	12 sections --green onion
海參、花枝、菠菜 ------------	蒜片 --------------------- 8片	150g.(5⅓oz.) each ----sea	8 slices ----------------garlic
----------------各150公克	高湯 --------------------- 3杯	cucumber, squids,spinach	3C. ---------------------stock
蝦仁 ---------------- 60公克		60g.(2¹/₁₀oz.)--------shelled shrimp	

1
- 黑醋 ----------------- 3 大匙
- 醬油 ----------------- 2 大匙
- 酒、麻油 --------各 1 大匙
- 糖 ---------------------½小匙
- 鹽、味精 --------各¼小匙

2
- 水 ----------------- 4 大匙
- 太白粉 ------------- 2 大匙

1
- •3T.brown vinegar
- •2T.soy sauce
- •1T.each cooking wine, sesame oil
- •½t.sugar
- •¼t.salt

2
- •4T.water
- •2T.corn starch

1 海參去腸泥洗淨，切成3公分長條狀，菠菜洗淨切4公分段。
2 花枝洗淨，切3×3公分花刀片狀，蝦仁洗淨備用。
3 鍋熱入油2大匙燒熱，入蔥段、蒜片爆香，續入花枝、海參、蝦仁略炒，最後入高湯及**1**料煮開，再入菠菜煮熟後以**2**料芶芡，淋於白飯上即可。

1 Remove entrails and wash sea cucumber, cut into 3 cm (1⅕") long strips. Wash spinach and cut into 4 cm (1½") sections.
2 Wash squids, cut into 3 cm x 3 cm (1⅕" x 1⅕") serving pieces. Wash shrimp.
3 Heat the wok, add 2T. oil and heat; stir fry green onion sections and garlic slices until fragrant. Add squids, sea cucumber, and shrimp to fry slightly. Pour in stock and **1**, bring to a boil. Add spinach, boil until cooked. Thicken with **2**. Pour over rice and serve.

家常燴飯 • *Rice with Home Style Sauce*

白飯 -------------- 1 0 0 0公克　　胡蘿蔔、熟青豆仁 各6 0公克
里肌肉、洋蔥 --- 各1 5 0公克　　香菇 --------------------- 1 0公克
熟筍 ------------------- 1 3 0公克

1 ┌ 水 ------------------- 2 小匙
　　├ 醬油、太白粉 -- 各1 小匙
　　└ 酒 ------------------- ½小匙

2 ┌ 水 ------------------- 4 杯
　　├ 糖 ------------------- 2 小匙
　　└ 鹽 ------------------- 1 小匙

3 ┌ 醬油 ----------------- 2 大匙
　　├ 黑醋 ----------------- 1 大匙
　　├ 麻油 ----------------- 1 小匙
　　├ 味精 ----------------- ½小匙
　　└ 胡椒粉 -------------- ¼小匙

4 太白粉、水 ------- 各2 大匙

1 里肌肉逆紋切絲，加 **1** 料醃1 0分鐘；香菇先泡軟再與洋蔥、筍、胡蘿蔔均切絲備用；白飯先置於碗內。

2 鍋熱入油1 ½大匙燒熱，入肉絲炒熟盛起，餘油先炒香洋蔥，再入香菇、筍、胡蘿蔔及 **2** 料煮開後續煮2分鐘，再入肉絲、青豆仁及 **3** 料煮開並以 **4** 料芶芡，淋於白飯上即可。

1000g.(2⅕lb.) ----- cooked rice
150g.(5⅓oz.) each --- pork fillet, onion
130g.(4⅗oz.) ---- bamboo shoots

60g.(2¹/₁₀oz.)each - carrots, boiled green peas
10g.(⅓oz.) ------------ dried black mushrooms

1 ┌ •2t.water
　　├ •1t.each soy sauce, corn starch
　　└ •½t.cooking wine

2 ┌ •4C.water
　　├ •2t.sugar
　　└ •1t.salt

3 ┌ •2T.soy sauce
　　├ •1T.brown vinegar
　　├ •1t.sesame oil
　　└ •¼t.pepper

4 ┌ •2T.each corn starch, water

1 Shred pork across the grain, and marinate in **1** for 10 minutes.　Soften mushrooms in warm water, discard stems. Shred mushrooms, onion, bamboo shoots, and carrots. Place rice in a large bowl.

2 Heat 1½T. oil, stir fry pork and remove. In the remaining oil, stir fry onion until fragrant, add mushrooms, bamboo shoots, carrots, and **2**. Bring to a boil and simmer for 2 minutes. Then add pork, peas, and **3**; thicken with **4**.　Pour over rice and serve.

咖哩燴飯 • *Rice with Curry Pork Sauce*

白飯 -------------- 1 0 0 0 公克	胡蘿蔔 -------------- 8 0 公克	1000g.(2⅕lb.) ----- cooked rice	130g.(4³⁄₅oz.) ---- potatoes
里肌肉 -------------- 1 8 0 公克	麵粉 ---------------- 3 大匙	180g.(6¹⁄₃oz.) --- pork fillet	80g.(2⁴⁄₅oz.) -------- carrots
洋蔥 ---------------- 1 5 0 公克	咖哩粉 -------------- 2 大匙	150g.(5¹⁄₃oz.) -------- onion	3T. ---------------------- flour
馬鈴薯 -------------- 1 3 0 公克			2T. ----------- curry powder

1 醬油、太白粉 ---- 各 2 小匙

2
- 水 ------------------ 3 杯
- 酒 ------------------ 1 大匙
- 鹽、糖 ----------- 各 2 小匙
- 胡椒粉 -------------- ¼ 小匙

1
- •2t.each soy sauce, corn starch

2
- •3C.water
- •1T.cooking wine
- •2t.each salt, sugar
- •¼t.pepper

1 里肌肉、胡蘿蔔、洋蔥、馬鈴薯均切 1 公分小丁，肉丁入 **1** 料拌醃。

2 鍋熱入油 4 大匙燒熱，入肉丁炒至變色後盛起，留油再入胡蘿蔔、馬鈴薯略炒盛起備用。

3 鍋洗淨再入油 6 大匙燒熱，入洋蔥炒香，隨入咖哩粉、麵粉略炒，再加胡蘿蔔、馬鈴薯及 **2** 料煮開後，改小火待馬鈴薯煮熟後，再入肉丁煮開即可淋於飯上。

1 Cut pork, carrots, onion, and potatoes into 1 cm (²⁄₅") dice. Marinate pork with **1**.

2 Heat the wok, add 4T. oil and heat; stir fry pork until color changes, remove. Add carrots and potatoes to fry for a while, then remove.

3 In a clean wok, add 6T. oil and heat; stir fry onion until fragrant. Add curry powder and flour to fry, then add carrots, potatoes, and **2**; bring to a boil and simmer over low heat until potatoes are done. Stir in pork and bring to a boil again. Pour over rice and serve.

雞肉羹飯 • *Chicken Pottage Over Rice*

白飯 -------------- 1000公克	金針 -------------------- 15公克
青江菜 -------------- 200公克	乾木耳 -------------------- 5公克
雞肉 ----------------- 150公克	蛋 -------------------------- 2個

1 ⎡ 太白粉 ------------ 1小匙
⎢ 鹽、糖、麻油 --- 各½小匙
⎢ 味精 ---------------- ¼小匙
⎣ 胡椒粉 ------------- ⅛小匙

3 太白粉、水 ------ 各2大匙

2 ⎡ 高湯 -------------------- 5杯
⎢ 鹽、糖 ----------- 各1小匙
⎣ 味精 ---------------- ½小匙

4 ⎡ 蒜末、醬油 ----- 各1大匙
⎢ 麻油 ---------------- 1小匙
⎣ 胡椒粉 ------------- ½小匙

1 雞肉切片，入 **1** 料拌醃；金針泡軟去梗打結；木耳泡軟去蒂切片；青江菜燙熟漂涼後切半；蛋打散備用。

2 **2** 料煮開，將雞肉一片一片放入後，續入金針、木耳、青江菜煮開，以 **3** 料芶芡，再把蛋液徐徐加入，立即熄火，隨入 **4** 料調味，即為雞肉羹湯，淋在飯上即可。

1000g.(2⅕lb.) ----- cooked rice	15g.(½oz.) -------- dried lily flowers
200g.(7oz.) ------ bok choy	5g.(⅕oz.) ------ dried black wood ears
150g.(5⅓oz.) ------ chicken breast	2 ------------------------ eggs

1 ⎡ • 1t .corn starch
⎢ • ½t.each salt, sugar, sesame oil
⎣ • ⅛t.pepper

3 ⎡ • 2T.each corn starch, water

2 ⎡ • 5C.stock
⎣ • 1t.each salt, sugar

4 ⎡ • 1T.each soy sauce, minced garlic
⎢ • 1t.sesame oil
⎣ • ½t.pepper

1 Slice chicken and marinate in **1**; soften dried lily flowers and black wood ears in water, then discard the hard stems. Cook bok choy in boiling water, rinse under cold water; cut to halves. Beat the eggs.

2 Bring **2** to a boil, add chicken slices, continue with dried lily flowers, wood ears, and bok choy. Bring to a boil again, thicken with **3**. Slowly pour in beaten eggs. Shut off the heat immediately and season with **4**. This is the chicken pottage. Pour over rice and serve.

菠蘿炒飯

Pineapple Fried Rice

二人份　　**serve 2**

菠蘿炒飯 · *Pineapple Fried Rice*

白飯	----------------	６００公克
蝦仁	----------------	１００公克
香腸	----------------	７０公克
熟青豆仁	--------------	４０公克
香菇	----------------	６公克
蛋	----------------	２個
鳳梨	----------------	１個
蔥末	----------------	８大匙

1
鹽	----------------	1小匙
味精	----------------	½小匙
胡椒粉	----------------	¼小匙

1 鳳梨對半剖開，取一半挖出鳳梨肉後，洗淨瀝乾。

2 取１００公克鳳梨肉切成小丁，蝦仁洗淨瀝乾水分，香腸切薄片，香菇泡軟切丁，蛋打散備用。

3 鍋熱入油１大匙燒熱，入蛋液炒熟盛出，再入油 ½ 大匙燒熱，炒香蔥末，入蝦仁、香腸炒熟盛出，餘油入香菇炒香後，續入白飯炒勻，再入 **1** 料、蝦仁、香腸、鳳梨、蛋和青豆仁並炒勻，隨即盛起置於鳳梨殼上即可。

■ 鳳梨之多寡可隨自己喜好而增減。

600g.(1⅓lb.)	--cooked rice
1	----------------------------------pineapple (with rind)
100g.(3½oz.)	---------------------------------shelled shrimp
1 (70g. or 2½oz.)	------------------------------------sausage
40g.(1⅖oz.) each	------boiled green peas,minced green onion
6g.(⅕oz.)	----------------------------dried black mushrooms
2	---eggs

1
- 1t.salt
- ¼t.pepper

1 Cut pineapple into two halves lengthwise. Remove the edible flesh off one half, wash clean and pat dry the hollowed shell.

2 Dice 100g.(3½oz.) pineapple. Wash and pat dry the shrimp. Thinly slice the sausage. Soften mushrooms in warm water and dice. Beat eggs.

3 Heat the wok, add 1T. oil, stir fry the eggs quickly. Add ½T. more oil, stir fry white part of green onion until fragrant, add shrimp and sausage, fry until cooked, then remove. Stir in mushrooms, fry until fragrant; add rice, stir fry evenly. Then add **1**, green part of green onion, shrimp, sausage, pineapple, eggs, and green peas; mix and heat well. Place in the hollowed pineapple shell and serve.

■ Amount of pineapple used depends on personal taste.

生炒牛肉飯 • *Fried Rice with Beef and Lettuce*

白飯 ----------------- 600公克	牛肉 ----------------- 150公克	600g.(1⅓lb.) - cooked rice	150g.(5¼oz.) --------- beef
西生菜 ------------- 200公克	蔥末 --------------------- 5大匙	200g.(7oz.)--------- lettuce	5T. -- minced green onion

1
- 水 ----------------- 3大匙
- 醬油 --------------- 1大匙
- 太白粉 ------------- 1小匙
- 酒 --------------------- ½小匙
- 小蘇打 ------------- ⅛小匙

2
- 醬油 ----------------- 2大匙
- 黑胡椒粉 ----------- ¼小匙
- 鹽、味精 -------- 各⅛小匙

1
- •3T.water
- •1T.soy sauce
- •1t.corn starch
- •½t.cooking wine
- •⅛t.baking soda

2
- •2T.soy sauce
- •¼t.pepper
- •⅛t.salt

1 牛肉切細絲入 **1** 料醃30分鐘後，入油鍋中過油至變色，隨即撈起，西生菜切細絲備用。

2 鍋熱入油2大匙燒熱，入蔥末炒香，隨入白飯及 **2** 料炒勻後，續入西生菜及牛肉拌勻即可。

1 Shred beef and marinate with **1** for 30 minutes. Place in hot oil until color changes, lift out immediately. Shred lettuce.

2 Heat the wok, add 2T. oil and heat; stir fry green onion until fragrant. Add rice and **2**, stir fry evenly. Mix in lettuce and beef.

青椒牛肉飯 ·*Green Pepper and Beef Fried Rice*

白飯 ----------------- ６００公克	蔥段 ----------------------- １４段
青椒、牛肉 ------ 各１５０公克	紅辣椒 ----------------------- 1條
薑絲 --------------------- ２０公克	

1
- 蛋液、油 -------- 各1大匙
- 醬油、水 -------- 各2小匙
- 太白粉 ------------- 1小匙
- 糖 --------------------½小匙

2
- 鹽 --------------------½小匙
- 味精、胡椒粉 --- 各¼小匙

1 牛肉逆紋切絲，入 **1** 料醃３０分鐘。
2 青椒、紅辣椒去籽切絲備用。
3 鍋熱入油１杯燒至六分熱（１４０℃），入牛肉絲炒熟盛起，鍋內留油３大匙燒熱，先炒香蔥、薑，再入紅辣椒、青椒炒熟，隨入白飯及 **2** 料炒勻，最後入牛肉絲拌勻即可。

600g.(1⅓lb.) - cooked rice
150g.(5⅓oz.) each - green peppers, beef
20g.(⅔oz.) -----shredded ginger
14 sections --green onion
1 ---------red chili pepper

1
- •1T.each beaten egg, oil
- •2t.each soy sauce, water
- •1t.corn starch
- •½t.sugar

2
- •½t.salt
- •¼t.pepper

1 Shred beef across the grain, and marinate in **1** for 30 minutes.
2 Discard the seeds and shred red and green peppers.
3 Heat the wok, add 1C. oil and heat to 140°C (284°F); stir fry shredded beef until cooked, remove. Keep 3T. oil in the wok and heat, stir fry green onion, ginger until fragrant. Add red chili pepper and green peppers, stir fry until cooked. Then add rice and **2**, stir fry and mix well. Mix in shredded beef and serve.

31

二人份　**serve 2**

番茄蛋炒飯 · *Tomato Fried Rice*

白飯 ------------ 600公克		番茄醬 ------------ 1 大匙
番茄 ------------ 120公克	**❶**	鹽 ------------ ¾小匙
蛋 ------------ 2 個		味精 ------------ ¼小匙
蔥末 ------------ 6 大匙		胡椒粉 ------------ ⅛小匙

1 番茄底部用刀在表皮劃一個十字（圖1），入開水中川燙 1 分鐘（圖2），取出去皮去蒂（圖3），切為四瓣並去籽，再切成 2 公分小丁，蛋打散成蛋液備用。

2 鍋熱入油 1½ 大匙燒熱，入蛋液炒成蛋花盛起，再入油 1½ 大匙燒熱，入蔥末爆香，再入番茄丁拌炒均勻，隨即入白飯、❶ 料及蛋花拌炒均勻即可。

600g.(1⅓lb.) - cooked rice		• 1T.ketchup
120g.(4¼oz.) --- tomatoes	**❶**	• ¾t.salt
2 ------------ eggs		• ⅛t.pepper
6T. --minced green onion		

1 Score a cross at the bottom of tomatoes (illus. 1), scald in boiling water for 1 minute (illus. 2), remove and peel off the skin (illus. 3); cut into quarters and discard the seeds. Then cut into 2 cm (¾") cubes. Beat the eggs.

2 Heat the wok, add 1½T. oil and heat; stir fry the eggs to softly scramble and remove. Add 1½T. oil into the wok and heat, stir fry minced green onion until fragrant, add tomatoes to fry. Mix in rice, ❶, and the eggs, heat thoroughly. Serve.

1

2

3

什錦炒飯 • *Mixed Fried Rice*

白飯 ---------------- 600公克	紅辣椒 ---------------------- 2條
香菇 ------------------- 6公克	蛋白 ------------------------- 少許
蔥末 ------------------- 6大匙	

1〔 洋火腿、胡蘿蔔、蒟蒻、
　　熟筍 ---------- 各50公克
　　魚板 ------------- 25公克

3 蛋白、太白粉 ------- 各少許

2〔 雞胸肉、蝦仁、熟毛豆仁
　　 ----------------- 各40公克
　　黃蘿蔔 ---------- 20公克

4〔 鹽 ---------------------- ³/₄小匙
　　味精、胡椒粉 --- 各¹/₄小匙

1 香菇泡軟去蒂，紅辣椒切開去籽均切丁。
2 **1**料均切成1公分立方小丁，胡蘿蔔、蒟蒻、筍入開水中燙熟備用。
3 雞胸肉、蝦仁均切丁，雞肉丁入 **3** 料拌醃；蝦仁丁入少許蛋白拌醃。
4 鍋熱入油 ½ 杯燒熱，入雞肉炒熟盛起，餘油續入蝦仁炒熟盛起備用。
5 鍋熱入油 2½ 大匙燒熱，入蔥末、香菇丁、紅辣椒丁及 **1** 料炒香，續入白飯及 **4** 料拌炒均勻，最後再加 **2** 料拌勻即可。

600g.(1⅓lb.) - cooked rice	6T. -- minced green onion
6g.(⅕oz.) ------ dried black mushrooms	2 --------- red chili peppers
	dash of ----------egg white

1〔 •50g.(1¾ oz.) each
　　ham,carrots,yam cake,
　　canned bamboo shoots
　　•25g.(⁸/₉oz.)kamaboko

2〔 •40g.(1²/₅oz.) each
　　chicken breast,shrimp,
　　boiled fresh soy beans
　　•20g.(²/₃oz.) yellow
　　turnip

3〔 •dash of each: egg
　　white, corn starch

4〔 •³/₄t.salt
　　•¹/₄t.pepper

1 Soften black mushrooms in water and discard the stems. Slice red chili peppers open, remove the seeds, and dice.
2 Cut all materials in **1** into 1 cm (²/₅") cubes. Boil carrots, yam cake, and bamboo shoots in boiling water until cooked, drain.
3 Dice chicken breast and shrimp. Marinate chicken with **3**, shrimp with a dash egg white.
4 Heat the wok, add ½C. oil and heat; stir fry chicken slightly and remove. In the remaining oil, stir fry shrimp until cooked, remove.
5 In a clean wok, add 2½T. oil and heat; stir fry green onion, mushrooms, red chili peppers, and **1** until fragrant. Add rice and **4**, stir fry evenly ; add **2** and mix well. Serve.

咖哩炒飯 • *Curry Fried Rice*

白飯 ----------------- ６００公克	熟青豆仁 -------------- ６０公克
里肌肉、洋蔥 --- 各１００公克	蔥末 ---------------------- ８大匙

1⎡ 醬油、太白粉 -- 各１小匙
　⎣ 酒 --------------------- ½小匙

2⎡ 咖哩粉 -------------- １大匙
　⎢ 鹽 --------------------- １小匙
　⎣ 味精 ----------------- ½小匙

1 里肌肉切１公分小丁，加 **1** 料略醃，洋蔥切丁備用。

2 鍋熱入油１大匙燒熱，入肉丁炒熟盛起，再加１大匙油炒香洋蔥、蔥末，並加 **2** 料略炒，隨入白飯炒勻，再入肉丁、青豆仁拌炒均勻即可。

600g.(1⅓lb.) - cooked rice
100g.(3½oz.) each --- pork fillet, onion

60g.(2¹⁄₁₀oz.) --------- boiled green peas
8T. --minced green onion

1⎡ •1t.each soy sauce, corn starch
　⎣ •½t.cooking wine

2⎡ •1T.curry powder
　⎣ •1t.salt

1 Dice pork into 1 cm (²⁄₅") cubes, marinate with **1** for a while. Dice onion.

2 Heat the wok, add 1T. oil and heat; stir fry pork until cooked, remove. Add 1T. oil into the wok, stir fry onion and minced green onion until fragrant, season with **2**, stir well. Mix in rice well, then add pork and green peas, stir well and heat thoroughly.

海南油雞飯 • *Hainan Chicken Rice*

雞腿 ----------------- 700公克	薑片 ------------------------ 3片	700g.(1½lb.) chicken legs	3 slices --------------- ginger
蓬萊米 -------------- 300公克	蒜末、酒 ------------- 各1大匙	300g.(10½oz.) ------- short grain rice	1T.each ---- minced garlic, cooking wine
蔥段 ------------------------ 5段		5 sections ---- green onion	

1┌ 鹽 ------------------- ½小匙
　└ 胡椒粉 ------------- ⅛小匙

2┌ 醬油 ---------------- 2大匙
　├ 蔥末、薑末 ------ 各½大匙
　└ 麻油 ------------------- 少許

1┌ •½t.salt
　└ •⅛t.pepper

2┌ •2T.soy sauce
　├ •½T.each minced green onion,minced ginger
　└ •dash of sesame oil

1 雞腿洗淨，入開水中川燙以去血水，取出洗淨，另加水7杯及蔥、薑、酒大火煮開改中火煮10分鐘，熄火燜10分鐘，取出雞肉，湯汁留2杯備用。

2 米洗淨，浸泡1小時後瀝乾。鍋熱入油2大匙燒熱，入蒜末炒香，續入米拌炒均勻，再加雞湯1½杯及**1**料翻炒至半熟時，盛入電鍋內鍋中，再加雞湯½杯，電鍋外鍋加水½杯，煮至電鍋跳起，續燜5分鐘後取出。

3 **2**料調勻當雞肉沾汁，雞肉切塊配以米飯食用即為海南油雞飯。

1 Wash chicken legs, parboil in boiling water to rid off blood, remove and rinse. Add chicken legs into 7C. water and green onion sections, ginger slices and cooking wine, bring to boiling over high heat. Turn heat to medium and simmer for 10 minutes, turn off heat and let it remain covered for extra 10 minutes. Remove chicken. Keep 2C. soup for later use.

2 Rinse rice, soak in water for 1 hour, drain. Heat the wok, add 2T. oil and heat; stir fry minced garlic until fragrant, add rice and mix well. Pour in 1½C. chicken soup and **1**, stir fry until the rice is half-cooked. Place rice into a rice cooker, add the remaining ½C. chicken soup into the rice and ½C. water into the outer pot, boil until the rice cooker shuts off. Let it remain covered for extra 5 minutes. Remove.

3 Mix **2** well to be the dipping sauce for chicken. Cut chicken legs into serving pieces and serve with the rice.

肉絲炒飯 · *Fried Rice with Shredded Pork*

白飯 ----------------- ６００公克　　蔥 ------------------------- 4 枝
瘦豬肉 ------------- １５０公克

1
- 水 ------------------- 2 大匙
- 醬油 ---------------- 1 大匙
- 太白粉 ------------- 2 小匙

2
- 鹽 ------------------ 1 小匙
- 味精 --------------- ½小匙
- 胡椒粉 ------------- ¼小匙

1 豬肉逆紋切成細絲，入 **1** 料拌勻醃１０分鐘，蔥洗淨切絲。
2 鍋熱入油３大匙燒熱，入肉絲炒熟後撈出，餘油再入蔥絲炒香，
　　隨即入白飯、**2** 料炒拌均勻，再入肉絲拌勻即可。

600g.(1⅓lb.) -cooked rice　　4 -------------- green onions
150g.(5⅓oz.) ---lean pork

1
- 2T.water
- 1T.soy sauce
- 2t.corn starch

2
- 1t.salt
- ¼t.pepper

1 Shred pork across the grain, marinate with **1** for 10 minutes. Wash green onions and shred.
2 Heat the wok, add 3T. oil and heat; stir fry shredded pork until cooked, then remove. In the remaining oil, stir fry green onions until fragrant, add rice and **2**, mix well. Stir in shredded pork and serve.

二人份　　**serve 2**

火腿蛋炒飯 · *Fried Rice with Ham and Eggs*

白飯 ----------------- ６００公克
火腿、熟青豆仁 ---各８０公克
蛋 ------------------------- 2 個
蔥末 ---------------------- 3 大匙

1
- 鹽 ------------------ 1 小匙
- 味精 --------------- ½小匙
- 胡椒粉 ------------- ¼小匙

1 火腿切薄片，再切成１公分之小方塊備用。
2 鍋熱入油 1½ 大匙燒熱，入打散之蛋液炒熟盛起。
3 鍋再熱入油 1 大匙燒熱，炒香蔥末及火腿，續入白飯、**1** 料炒勻
　　後，再入蛋、青豆仁拌勻即可。

600g.(1⅓lb.) -cooked rice
80g.(2⅘oz.) each ---ham, boiled green peas
2 ------------------------ eggs
3T. --minced green onion

1
- 1t.salt
- ¼t.pepper

1 Thinly slice the ham and cut into 1 cm (²⁄₅") small pieces.
2 Heat the wok, add 1½T. oil and heat; stir fry beaten eggs until cooked, remove.
3 Reheat the wok, add 1T. oil and heat; stir fry green onion and ham until fragrant. Add rice and **1**, mix well. Stir in fried eggs and peas, mix well and serve.

　　　　　二人份　　**serve 2**

鹹飯糰 · *Breakfast Rice Rolls*

長糯米 -------------- 100公克		糖 -------------------- ¼小匙
蘿蔔乾 ----------------- 30公克		胡椒粉 ---------------- 少許
肉鬆 -------------------- 25公克			
老油條 --------------------- ½條			

1 糯米洗淨煮成糯米飯，蘿蔔乾洗淨切碎備用。
2 鍋熱入油1小匙燒熱，入蘿蔔乾及 **1** 料炒勻盛起備用。
3 將所有材料分成2份，先取1份糯米飯平舖於塑膠袋上，再灑上
肉鬆、蘿蔔乾、最後放入油條，再將糯米飯捏合成橢圓形即可。

100g.(3½oz.) --long grain
glutinous rice
30g.(1oz.) ----dried turnip

25g.(⁸⁄₉oz.) ------seasoned
pork fiber
½ piece --------- deep fried
Chinese cruller

1 ⌐ •¼t.sugar
  └ •dash of pepper

1 Rinse rice and steam until cooked. Rinse turnip and
chop finely.
2 Heat the wok, add 1t. oil and heat; stir fry turnip and
1. remove.
3 Divide all materials into two equal portions, spread
one portion of cooked rice on a plastic sheet, sprinkle
on pork fibers and turnip, top with cruller. Pack
tightly into an oblong ball. Makes 2.

甜飯糰 · *Sweet Rice Rolls*

長糯米 -------------- 100公克		花生粉 ------------------ 20公克
細糖 ----------------------- 2大匙		老油條 ------------------------- ½條

1 糯米洗淨煮成糯米飯備用，花生粉、細糖先拌勻。
2 將所有材料分成2份，先取1份糯米飯平舖於塑膠袋上，再灑上
細糖、花生粉，最後放入油條，再把糯米飯捏合成橢圓形即可。

100g.(3½oz.) --long grain
glutinous rice
2T. --------------------sugar

20g.(²⁄₃oz.) ---------peanut
powder
½ piece --------- deep fried
Chinese cruller

1 Rinse rice and steam until cooked. Mix peanut
powder with sugar.
2 Divide all materials into 2 equal portions. Spread one
portion of rice on a plastic sheet, sprinkle on sugar
and peanut powder, top with cruller. Pack tightly into
an oblong ball. Makes 2.

三彩小飯糰 · *Tri-Colored Rice Balls*

白飯 ----------------- 600公克
雞胸肉、玉米粒 --- 各90公克
胡蘿蔔 ----------------- 60公克

1 ┌ 鹽 ----------------- 3/4小匙
　　└ 味精、胡椒粉 --- 各3/8小匙

1 雞胸肉、胡蘿蔔均切小細丁備用。
2 鍋熱入油3大匙燒熱，入雞胸肉炒熟，再入胡蘿蔔、玉米粒炒香，續入白飯及 **1** 料拌炒均勻，再分成24等份備用。
3 取1份炒飯捏緊成飯糰置於模型上，依序作即可。

600g.(1⅓lb.) - cooked rice
90g.(3⅕oz.) each ----------
chicken breast, corn
60g.(2¹/₁₀oz.) ------- carrots

1 ┌ • ¾t.salt
　　└ • ⅜t.pepper

1 Dice both chicken breast and the carrots.
2 Heat the wok, add 3T. oil and heat; stir fry chicken until cooked. Add carrots and corn, stir fry until fragrant. Mix in rice and **1** well. Divide into 24 equal portions.
3 Pack each portion into a ball by hand, makes 24.

翡翠小飯糰 · *Jade Rice Balls*

白飯、青江菜 --- 各600公克
筍 --------------------- 120公克
絞肉 --------------------- 90公克
鹽 ----------------------- 2大匙

1 ┌ 鹽 ----------------- 3/4小匙
　　└ 味精、胡椒粉 --- 各3/8小匙

1 青江菜洗淨瀝乾，加入鹽醃漬20分鐘後，漂洗去鹽分再切碎，擠乾水分；筍切細丁備用。
2 鍋熱入油3大匙燒熱，入絞肉炒熟，續入筍丁、青江菜炒香，入白飯及 **1** 料炒勻，再分成24等份備用。
3 取1份炒飯捏緊成飯糰置於模型上，依序作完即可。

600g.(1⅓lb.) each --------
cooked rice, bok choy
120g.(4¼oz.) ----bamboo
shoots
90g.(3⅕oz.) - ground pork
2T. -----------------------salt

1 ┌ • ¾t.salt
　　└ • ⅜t.pepper

1 Wash bok choy and drain, pickle in salt for 20 minutes. Rinse off the salt and chop finely, squeeze off the liquid. Dice bamboo shoots.
2 Heat the wok, add 3C. oil and heat; stir fry pork until cooked. Add diced bamboo shoots and bok choy, stir fry until fragrant. Stir in rice and **1**, mix well. Divide into 24 equal portions.
3 Pack each portion tightly into a rice ball by hand, makes 24.

叉燒小飯糰 • *Bar-B-Q Pork Rice Balls*

白飯 ------------------ ６００公克
叉燒肉 ------------------ ７５公克
洋火腿 ------------------ ６０公克
香菇 ---------------------- １２公克

1 鹽、味精、胡椒粉各³/₈小匙

1 香菇泡軟去蒂洗淨、與火腿、叉燒肉均切小細丁備用。
2 鍋熱入油３大匙燒熱，入香菇、火腿、叉燒肉炒香，再入白飯及 **1** 料炒勻，分成２４等份備用。
3 取１份炒飯捏緊成飯糰置於 模型上，依序作完即可。

600g.(1⅓lb.) - cooked rice
75g.(2⅔oz.) Bar-B-Q pork
60g.(2¹/₁₀oz.) ---------- ham
12g.(²/₅oz.) ---- dried black
mushrooms

1 • ³/₈t.each salt, pepper

1 Soften mushrooms in water, discard stems and rinse. Dice mushrooms, ham, and pork.
2 Heat the wok, add 3T. oil and heat; stir fry mushrooms, ham, and pork until fragrant. Add rice and **1**, mix well. Divide into 24 equal portions.
3 Pack each portion tightly into a ball by hand. Makes 24.

香蝦小飯糰 • *Shrimp Rice Balls*

白飯 ------------------ ６００公克
蝦仁 ------------------ １５０公克
筍 ------------------ １２０公克
香菇 ------------------ １２公克
蔥末 ------------------ ３大匙

1 鹽 -------------------- ³/₄小匙
味精、胡椒粉 --- 各³/₈小匙

1 香菇泡軟去蒂洗淨、與筍、蝦仁均切小細丁備用。
2 鍋熱入油３大匙燒熱，入蔥末爆香，續入蝦仁、香菇、筍炒熟，最後入白飯及 **1** 料炒勻，分成２４等份備用。
3 取１份炒飯捏緊成飯糰置於 模型上，依序作完即可。

600g.(1⅓lb.) - cooked rice
150g.(5⅓oz.) ------ shelled shrimp
120.(4¼oz.) ------ bamboo shoots

12g.(²/₅oz.) ---- dried black mushrooms
3T. -- minced green onion

1 • ³/₄t.salt
• ³/₈t.pepper

1 Soften mushrooms in water, discard the stems, and rinse. Dice mushrooms, bamboo shoots, and shrimp.
2 Heat the wok, add 3T. oil and heat; stir fry green onion until fragrant. Add shrimp, mushrooms, and bamboo shoots, stir fry until cooked. Mix in rice and **1** well. Remove and divide into 24 equal portions.
3 Pack each portion tightly into a ball by hand, makes 24.

米飯三明治 · *Rice Sandwich*

白飯 ----------------- ７００公克	香鬆 -------------------- 1½大匙	700g.(1½lb.) - cooked rice	25g.(1oz.)------------onion
罐頭鮪魚 -------------- ５０公克	正方盒（１５公分×１５公分	50g.(1¾oz.) canned tuna in spring water	1T. ---seaweed seasoning
肉鬆 ----------------- ４０公克	） ------------------------- 1個	40g.(1²/₅oz.)-----seasoned pork fiber	1 ---------------- square box (15 cm x 15 cm / 6" x 6")
洋蔥 ----------------- ２５公克			

１⎰ 沙拉醬 ---------- ２５公克
⎱ 黑胡椒粉、鹽、白醋 -----
-------------------- 各⅛小匙

1 洋蔥切細丁，加攪碎鮪魚及**１**料調勻即為鮪魚沙拉。
2 正方盒先鋪上一層保鮮膜，第一層先入白飯２００公克鋪平，第二層入肉鬆抹勻（圖１），第三層入白飯１５０公克鋪平（圖２），第四層入鮪魚沙拉抹平，第五層入白飯１５０公克鋪平，第六層均勻灑上香鬆，第七層入白飯２００公克鋪平並壓緊，然後將整盒飯取出，切成１６塊即為米飯三明治。

１⎰ •25g.(1oz.) mayonnaise
⎱ •⅛t.each pepper, salt, white vinegar

1 Chop onion into fine dice, mix with tuna and **１**.
2 Line the square box with a sheet of saran wrap. Spread 200g.(7oz.) rice evenly, then add a layer of pork fiber (illus. 1). The third layer is 150g.(5⅓ oz.) rice (illus. 2). The tuna mixture is the fourth layer and it too is spread evenly. Again, spread the fifth layer with 150g.(5⅓oz.) rice, then sprinkle on seaweed seasoning evenly as the sixth layer. Top with a seventh layer of 200g.(7oz.) rice, spread evenly and press tightly down. Remove the whole sandwich layers out of the box carefully. Cut into 16 serving pieces. Serve.

1

2

炒飯壽司 • *Fried Rice Sushi Rolls*

白飯 ---------------- 200公克	紫菜 ------------------------ 3 片	200g.(7oz.) --- cooked rice	3 sheets ---------- seaweed
雞胸肉 --------------- 50公克	蛋 -------------------------- 2 個	50g.(1¾oz.) ------ chicken breast	2 ------------------------ eggs
胡蘿蔔 --------------- 30公克	小黃瓜 ---------------------- 1 條	30g.(1oz.) ---------- carrots	1 ---------- baby cucumber
青豆仁 --------------- 20公克	蔥末 ----------------------- 1 大匙	20g.(²/₃oz.) ---- green peas	1T. -- minced green onion

1 ┌ 蛋白 ---------------- 1 小匙
　　└ 鹽 ----------------- ⅛小匙

2 ┌ 鹽 --------------------- ¼小匙
　　└ 味精、胡椒粉 --- 各⅛小匙

1 ┌ •1t. egg white
　　└ •⅛t. salt

2 ┌ •¼t. salt
　　└ •⅛t. pepper

1 雞胸肉、胡蘿蔔、小黃瓜均切細丁，雞胸肉加 **1** 料拌醃 5 分鐘，蛋打散備用。

2 鍋熱入油 1 大匙燒熱，入雞胸肉炒熟盛起，另入油 1 大匙燒熱，入蛋液炒成蛋花盛起，另再入油 1 大匙燒熱，入蔥末炒香，續入胡蘿蔔、小黃瓜、白飯及 **2** 料炒勻，最後入雞胸肉、蛋花、青豆仁拌勻即為炒飯，分成 3 等份。

3 紫菜置於竹簾上，取 1 份炒飯平舖於紫菜上（圖 1），捲成壽司（圖 2），其餘 2 份作法相同，再切片即可。

1 Cut chicken, carrots, and cucumber into small dice. Marinate chicken with **1** for 5 minutes. Beat the eggs.

2 Heat the wok, add 1T. oil and heat; stir fry chicken until cooked, then remove. Add 1T. oil and heat, stir fry beaten eggs until softly scrambled, remove. Add 1T. oil again and heat, stir fry minced green onion until fragrant. Add carrots, cucumber, rice and **2**, mix well. Then add chicken, eggs, and peas, stir evenly. Remove and divide into 3 equal portions.

3 Place one sheet of seaweed on a bamboo screen sheet, spread one portion of fried rice on top (illus. 1), roll it into sushi roll (illus. 2). Makes 3. Slice into serving pieces and serve.

1

2

41

酒釀雞湯 • *Chicken and Wine Rice Soup*

雞腿 ------------------ 300公克
香菇 -------------------- 10公克
紅棗 --------------------------- 6個
蔥段 --------------------------- 4段
薑 ----------------------------- 2片
酒釀 ------------------------ 4大匙
鹽 --------------------------- 1小匙

1 雞腿洗淨切3×3公分塊狀，香菇泡軟去蒂切塊，紅棗洗淨備用。
2 將雞肉、香菇、紅棗、蔥段、薑片、酒釀置燉盅內加水3杯，入蒸鍋蒸40分鐘，取出加鹽拌勻即可。

300g.($10\frac{1}{2}$oz.) ---- chicken legs
10g.($\frac{1}{3}$oz.) ----- dried black mushrooms
6 ----- dried Chinese dates
4 sections ---- green onion
2 slices --------------- ginger
4T. -- fermented wine rice
1t. ------------------------ salt

1 Wash chicken legs, cut into 3 cm x 3 cm ($1\frac{1}{5}$" x $1\frac{1}{5}$") pieces. Soften mushrooms in water, discard stems, and cut into small pieces. Wash dates.
2 Place chicken, mushrooms, dates, green onion sections, ginger slices, and fermented wine rice in a serving ceramic pot, add 3C. water. Steam for 40 minutes, season with salt, and serve directly from the steamer.

酒釀燒雞 • *Wine Rice Braised Chicken*

雞腿 ------------------ 600公克
酒釀 ------------------------ 5大匙
醬油 ------------------------ 3大匙
鹽 --------------------------- ¼小匙
蔥段 --------------------------- 8段
蒜頭 --------------------------- 2個

1 雞腿洗淨切3×3公分塊狀，蒜頭切片備用。
2 鍋熱入油2大匙燒熱，入蒜頭、蔥段爆香，續入雞塊炒至變色（約2分鐘），再入醬油、鹽、酒釀3大匙及水1杯煮開後，改小火煮至湯汁快收乾（約15分鐘）再入酒釀2大匙拌炒均勻即可。

600g.($1\frac{1}{3}$lb.) chicken legs
5T. -- fermented wine rice
3T. ---------------- soy sauce
$\frac{1}{4}$t. ------------------------ salt
8 sections ---- green onion
2 cloves --------------- garlic

1 Wash chicken, cut into 3 cm x 3 cm ($1\frac{1}{5}$" x $1\frac{1}{5}$") pieces. Slice garlic.
2 Heat the wok, add 2T. oil and heat; stir fry garlic and green onion sections until fragrant. Add chicken pieces and stir fry until color pales (about 2 minutes). Mix in soy sauce, salt, 3T. fermented wine rice, and 1C. water, bring to a boil. Simmer over low heat until sauce reduced to nearly nothing (about 15 minutes), stir in 2T. fermented wine rice. Mix well and serve.

珍珠丸子 · *Pearl Balls*

絞肉 ------------------ 2 0 0公克	
長糯米 -------------- 1 2 0公克	**1** [酒、麻油 -------- 各1小匙
荸薺 --------------------- 6 0公克	鹽、味精 -------- 各¼小匙
香菜 ------------------------- 1棵	

1 長糯米洗淨，泡水 5 0分鐘瀝乾備用。

2 荸薺切碎，與絞肉及 **1** 料拌勻，用力甩打數下後，擠成如乒乓球大小的肉丸，再沾裹長糯米入鍋大火蒸 2 0分鐘，取出飾以洗淨的香菜葉即可。

200g.(7oz.) - ground pork
120g.(4¼oz.) -- long grain glutinous rice
60g.(2¹/₁₀oz.) --------- water chestnuts
1 ------------------ coriander

1 [• 1t.each cooking wine, sesame oil
   • ¼t.salt

1 Rinse rice, soak in water for 50 minutes, drain.

2 Chop water chestnuts finely, mix well with pork and season with **1**. Throw and beat the mixture against the container for a few times. Squeeze the mixture into ping-pong size balls, roll the balls with rice. Steam over high heat for 20 minutes. Decorate with coriander and serve.

糯米糕 · *Glutinous Rice Cake*

圓糯米 -------------- 4 0 0公克	酒 ------------------------- 2大匙
桂圓肉 -------------- 1 0 0公克	玻璃紙 ----------------------- 1張
二砂紅糖 --------------------¾杯	

1 糯米洗淨，煮成糯米飯，取出趁熱加酒、桂圓肉及糖拌勻，再入電鍋中蒸5分鐘。

2 取一小鋁盤，舖上玻璃紙，上擦少許油，再把糯米飯舖上壓緊，待完全冷卻後再切食。

■1 亦可用玻璃紙置於竹簾上，再舖上糯米飯，便於壓緊。

2 桂圓肉亦可以芝麻、葡萄乾等代替。

400g.(14oz.) -- short grain glutinous rice
100g.(3½oz.) --------- dried longans

¾C. ---------- brown sugar
2T. ---------- cooking wine
1 sheet - cellophane paper

1 Wash rice, mix with 1C. water and 1T. wine; steam in rice cooker until done. Mix in sugar while warm, steam again for 5 minutes.

2 Spead cellophane paper on small baking tins, grease with a little oil; press in rice tightly. After thoroughly cold, slice and serve.

■1 Cellophane paper may be placed on a bamboo screen sheet, put rice on paper, and roll tightly.

2 Dried longan may be replaced by sesame seeds or raisins.

涼糕 · *Chilled Rice Cake*

圓糯米	200公克	白芝麻	3大匙
豆沙	50公克	豬油、酸梅粉	各1大匙
細糖	¼杯		

1 圓糯米洗淨煮成糯米飯，趁熱加糖及豬油拌勻待涼。

2 白芝麻炒香、搗碎，加酸梅粉拌勻。

3 取一竹簾，上置保鮮膜，抹上少許沙拉油（圖1），將糯米飯平舖其上，灑上2項之材料，放上豆沙壓平（圖2），再將竹簾對折壓緊（圖3），入冰箱冰涼後即可切塊食用。

200g.(7oz.) --- short grain glutinous rice
50g.(1¾oz.)` --- sweet red bean paste

¼C. -------------------- sugar
3T. ----------- sesame seeds
1T.each -- lard, sour prune powder

1 Rinse rice, and steam until cooked. Mix in sugar and lard while still warm.

2 Stir fry sesame seeds in a dry wok until fragrant, mix well with sour prune powder.

3 Line a bamboo rolling sheet with saran wrap, grease with a little salad oil (illus. 1). Spread rice evenly on top, sprinkle on step **2** ingredients, press on sweet red bean paste (illus. 2). Roll the bamboo rolling sheet tightly into a cylinder (illus. 3). Chill in the refrigerator until set, peel off the saran wrap, and cut into serving pieces.

1

2

3

八寶黑珍珠 • *Black Pearls with Candied Fruits*

黑糯米 -------------- 200公克	豆沙 -------------------- 60公克	200g.(7oz.) ----------- black glutinous rice 80g.(2⁴/₅oz.) --- long grain glutinous rice	60g.(2¹/₁₀oz.) ---- sweet red bean paste

1 ┌ 細糖 -------------------- ¼杯
　 └ 豬油 ----------------- 1大匙

2 ┌ 糖蓮子 ------------- 18顆
　 │ 糖酥腰果 ---------- 14顆
　 │ 蜜糖白果 ------------ 6顆
　 │ 綠櫻桃 --------------- 3顆
　 │ 紅櫻桃 --------------- 1顆
　 └ 芒果乾 ---------------- 少許

1 •¼C.sugar
　 •1T.lard

2 ┌ •18 candied lotus seeds
　 │ •14 sugar-coated cashew nuts
　 │ •6 candied ginkgo nuts
　 │ •3 candied green cherries
　 │ •1 candied red cherries
　 └ •as needed candied mango

1 黑糯米、長糯米洗淨泡水4小時，瀝乾水分，倒入電鍋內鍋加水1½杯，外鍋加水½杯煮至電鍋跳起，續燜10分鐘，取出與 **1** 料拌勻分成2份，豆沙略壓扁備用。

2 中碗1個，內舖一層保鮮膜，先以 **2** 料排圖案（圖1），再舖上1份黑糯米飯（圖2），中間舖上豆沙，上面再填上另1份黑糯米飯壓緊，入電鍋蒸10分鐘，取出倒扣於盤中即可。

1 Rinse black and long grain glutinous rice, soak in water for 4 hours, drain. Place rice in a rice cooker, add 1 ½C. water. Add ½C. water into the outer pot, cook until rice cooker shuts off. Continue simmering with lid on for 10 extra minutes. Remove, mix well with **1** and divide into two equal portions.

2 Line a medium size bowl with saran wrap, arrange materials in **2** into a geometric design (illus. 1). Spread a portion of rice evenly on top (illus. 2), spread the center with sweet red bean paste and press even. Top with another layer of rice and press even. Steam in rice cooker for 10 minutes. Invert onto a plate and serve.

1

2

45

二人份　serve 2

鹹飯 · *Salted Rice*

蓬萊米 -------------- 200公克	熟青豆仁 -------------- 15公克
里肌肉、芋頭------ 各50公克	蝦米 --------------------- 10公克
熟筍、胡蘿蔔------ 各30公克	香菇 ----------------------- 4公克
紅蔥頭 ------------------ 20公克	

❶ ┌ 水 ------------------------- ¼杯
　　├ 醬油 ----------------- 1大匙
　　├ 鹽 --------------------- ½小匙
　　├ 味精 ----------------- ¼小匙
　　└ 胡椒粉 -------------- ⅛小匙

1 米洗淨，里肌肉、芋頭、筍、胡蘿蔔切丁，紅蔥頭切片，蝦米洗淨泡水瀝乾，香菇泡軟切丁，均備用。

2 鍋熱入油2大匙燒熱，入紅蔥頭及蝦米炒香，續入肉丁、芋頭、筍、胡蘿蔔、香菇及 **❶** 料炒勻，再入洗淨的米同炒均勻，倒入電鍋內鍋中並加水1杯，外鍋加水 ½ 杯，入電鍋煮至跳起再燜5分鐘，再拌入青豆仁即可。

200g.(7oz.) --- short grain rice
50g.(1¾oz.) each ---- pork fillet, taros
30g.(1oz.) each --- boiled bamboo shoots, carrots
20g.(⅔oz.) ---- red shallots

15g.(½oz.) --- boiled green peas
10g.(⅓oz.) ----- dried baby shrimp
4g.(⅐oz.) ------ dried black mushrooms

❶ ┌ •¼C.water
　　├ •1T.soy sauce
　　├ •½t.salt
　　└ •⅛t.pepper

1 Wash rice. Dice pork, taros, bamboo shoots, and carrots. Slice shallots. Soften shrimp and mushrooms in water; and dice mushrooms.

2 Heat 2T. oil, stir fry shallots and shrimp until fragrant. Add pork, taros, bamboo shoots, carrots, mushrooms, and **❶**, mix well. Then add rice, stir fry together evenly. Place in rice cooker, add 1C. water into the rice, and ½C. water into the outer pot, cook until the rice cooker shuts off. Let it remain covered for 5 minutes extra. Remove, mix green peas before serving.

油飯 • *Mixed Rice a la Taiwanese*

長糯米 -------------- 2００公克　　蝦米 --------------------- 1０公克
里肌肉 ----------------- 4０公克　　香菇 ----------------------- 4 公克
紅蔥頭、乾魷魚 ---各2０公克

1　醬油 -------------- 1½大匙
　　鹽、味精、麻油 各¼小匙
　　胡椒粉 -------------- ⅛小匙

1 長糯米洗淨，加水 ⅘ 杯煮成糯米飯備用。
2 里肌肉逆紋切絲，紅蔥頭切片，香菇泡軟切絲，乾魷魚剪成條狀連同蝦米洗淨泡軟瀝乾備用。
3 鍋熱入油２大匙燒熱，入紅蔥頭、蝦米、香菇絲爆香，續入肉絲、魷魚絲及 **1** 料炒熟，再入糯米飯拌勻即可。

190g.(6⅔oz.) -- long grain glutinous rice
40g.(1⅖oz.) ---- pork fillet
20g.(⅔oz.) each ------- red shallots, dried cuttlefish

10g.(⅓oz.) ----- dried baby shrimp
4g.(⅐oz.) ------ dried black mushrooms

1　• 1½T. soy sauce
　　• ¼t. each salt, sesame oil
　　• ⅛t. pepper

1 Wash rice, add ⅘C. water, steam in rice cooker.
2 Shred pork fillet across the grain; slice shallots. Soften mushrooms in warm water, discard stems, and shred. Cut cuttlefish into long strips, soak in water. Wash shrimp and soak in water.
3 Heat 2T. oil, stir fry shallots, shrimp, and mushrooms until fragrant. Add pork, cuttlefish, and **1**, fry until cooked. Then add cooked rice, mix well and serve.

粉蒸排骨 • *Steamed Ribs with Rice Powder*

小排骨、地瓜 --- 各 2 2 5 公克 五香蒸肉粉 ------------- 3½ 大匙 蔥末 ---------------------- 2 大匙	**1** 油、水 ----------- 各 1 大匙 醬油、酒、糖、辣豆瓣醬 、甜麵醬、麻油 各½ 大匙 蔥末、薑末 ----- 各 1 小匙 味精 ----------------- ¼ 小匙 花椒粉 --------------- ⅛ 小匙

1 小排骨加 **1** 料醃 3 0 分鐘，地瓜去皮洗淨切滾刀塊。

2 將醃好的小排骨加五香蒸肉粉拌勻，入扣碗底部（圖 1），剩餘湯汁與地瓜拌勻，置於小排骨上（圖 2），入鍋蒸約 1 小時至小排骨熟爛，取出倒扣，再灑上蔥末即可。

225g.(8oz.) each ---- baby pork ribs, sweet potatoes 3½T. ------------ five-spice-flavored rice powder 2T. -- minced green onion	**1** • 1T.each oil, water • ½T.each soy sauce, cooking wine, sugar, hot soy bean paste, sesame oil, sweet soy bean paste • 1t.each minced green onion,minced ginger • ⅛t.Szechwan pepper powder

1 Marinate baby pork ribs with **1** for 30 minutes. Wash sweet potatoes and cut into slanting pieces.

2 Coat ribs with five-spice-flavored rice powder and arrange in a large bowl (illus 1). Mix remaining marinate sauce with sweet potato pieces, arrange sweet potatoes on top of the ribs (illus. 2). Steam in a steamer for 1 hour until ribs are tender. Invert onto a plate, sprinkle on minced green onion and serve.

1

2

魯肉飯 • *Rice with Pork Shallot Sauce*

下肉 ---------------- 3 0 0公克

1 ┌ 蓬萊米 -------- 4 0 0公克
　　│ 長糯米 --------- 9 5公克
　　│ 水 ------------------ 2½杯
　　└ 油 ------------------ 1 大匙

2 ┌ 紅蔥頭末 ---------- 3 大匙
　　└ 蒜末、薑末 ------ 各½大匙

3 ┌ 水 ---------------------- 5 杯
　　│ 酒 ---------------------- ½杯
　　│ 醬油 --------------------- ¼杯
　　│ 麻油 ----------------- 2 大匙
　　│ 冰糖、黑醋 ----- 各1 大匙
　　│ 味精 ----------------- ½小匙
　　│ 肉桂粉、五香粉、甘草粉
　　└ 、胡椒粉 --------- 各⅛小匙

1 下肉先入水中煮熟後切細絲。
2 **1** 料入電鍋中煮成飯備用。
3 鍋熱入油 2 大匙燒熱，入 **2** 料爆香，續入肉絲及 **3** 料煮開，改小火煮約 2 小時至肉熟爛，再淋於飯上即可。

300g.(10½oz.) -------- pork

1 •400g.(14oz.) short grain rice
　•95g.(3²/₅oz.) long grain glutinous rice
　•2½C.water
　•1T.oil

2 •3T.minced shallot
　•½T.each minced garlic, minced ginger

3 •5C.water
　•½C.cooking wine
　•¼C.soy sauce
　•2T.sesame oil
　•1T.each crystal sugar, brown vinegar
　•⅛t.each cinnamon powder,five spices powder, licorice powder, pepper

1 Boil pork until cooked, shred.
2 Place **1** in a rice cooker and cook the rice.
3 Heat the wok, add 2T. oil and heat; stir fry **2** until fragrant. Add shredded pork and **3**, bring to boiling. Turn heat to low and simmer for 2 hours. Pour sauce over rice and serve.

粟米粥 • *Congee with Corn*

蓬萊米 -------------- 200公克	紅棗 --------------------- 5粒
粟米粒（玉米）--- 140公克	薑片 --------------------- 9片
香菇 -------------------- 18公克	高湯 --------------------- 7杯

1 ┌ 薑片 --------------------- 6片
　　│ 油、水 ----------- 各2大匙
　　│ 酒 --------------------- ½大匙
　　└ 鹽、糖 ----------- 各¼小匙

2 ┌ 鹽、糖 ----------- 各1小匙
　　└ 胡椒粉 -------------- ¼小匙

1 香菇泡軟去蒂，每朵切成4等份，擠乾水分，加入 **1** 料入鍋蒸30分鐘，取出去薑片。

2 米洗淨，加油1大匙拌勻備用，粟米粒洗淨，用果汁機打成泥。

3 高湯煮開，入薑、紅棗、米以大火煮開，關小火續煮45分鐘，再入粟米泥煮10分鐘，最後再放入香菇、**2** 料拌勻即可。

200g.(7oz.) --- short grain rice	5 ----- dried Chinese dates
140g.(5oz.) ------------ corn	9 slices -------------- ginger
18g.(²/₃oz.) ---- dried black mushrooms	7C. ---------------------- stock

1 ┌ •6 slices ginger
　　│ •2T.each oil, water
　　│ •½T.cooking wine
　　└ •¼t.each salt, sugar

2 ┌ •1t.each salt, sugar
　　└ •¼t.pepper

1 Soften mushrooms in warm water, discard the stems; cut into quarters, squeeze out water and mix with **1**. Steam in a steamer for 30 minutes. Remove and discard ginger.

2 Wash rice, add 1T. oil, mix well. Wash corn and puree in a blender.

3 Bring stock to a boil, add ginger, dates, and rice. Bring to a boil over high heat, then simmer for 45 minutes. Add corn puree, and cook another 10 minutes. Add mushrooms and season with **2**. Mix well and serve.

絲瓜粥 ·*Sing Qua Congee*

絲瓜 ----------------- 800公克	高湯 ------------------------ 11杯
白飯 ----------------- 700公克	蔥段 ------------------------- 6段
瘦豬肉 -------------- 120公克	胡椒粉 ----------------------½小匙
蝦米 -------------------- 20公克	

1 ⎡ 鹽 ------------------- 2小匙
   ⎣ 味精 ----------------- ¼小匙

1 絲瓜去皮洗淨，與瘦肉均切1公分寬之薄片，蝦米洗淨，瀝乾備用。

2 鍋熱入油3大匙燒熱，入蔥段爆香，續入蝦米、瘦肉拌炒數下，隨入絲瓜炒軟，再入高湯、白飯煮開，最後入 **1** 料以小火燜煮約10分鐘，熄火，灑上胡椒粉即可。

800g.(1¾lb.) ----- sing qua	11C. ------------------- stock
700g.(1½lb.) - cooked rice	6 sections ---- green onion
120g.(4¼oz.) --- lean pork	½t. ------------------- pepper
20g.(⅔oz.) ----- dried baby shrimp	

1 •2t.salt

1 Skin sing qua and wash. Cut both sing qua and pork into 1 cm (⅖") wide thin slices. Wash dried shrimp and drain.

2 Heat the wok, add 3T. oil and heat; stir fry green onion sections until fragrant. Add dried shrimp and pork and fry slightly. Stir in sing qua slices to fry until softened. Pour in stock and rice, bring to a boil. Then season with **1**, simmer for 10 minutes. Turn off the heat, sprinkle on pepper. Serve.

台式鹹粥 · *Congee a la Taiwanese*

蓬萊米 -------------- ３００公克	花枝、生蠔 ----- 各１２０公克
絞肉 ----------------- ２００公克	高湯 ----------------------- １６杯
蘿蔔乾、芹菜末 各１６０公克	

１ 紅蔥頭 ----------- ７５公克
　　蝦米 ------------- ４０公克

２ 鹽 --------------------- ²/₃小匙
　　味精、胡椒粉 --- 各½小匙

1 花枝洗淨切花，蘿蔔乾切小丁，入水泡１０分鐘瀝乾，蝦米泡水瀝乾與紅蔥頭均切細末，生蠔洗淨瀝乾備用。

2 鍋熱入油４大匙燒熱，爆香 **１** 料，續入絞肉、蘿蔔乾，炒至香味出來，盛起備用。

3 米洗淨入高湯，大火煮開，改中火煮約１５分鐘，續入花枝、生蠔及 **2** 項材料，再以 **2** 料調味，起鍋後灑上芹菜末即可。

300g.(10½oz.) ------- short grain rice
200g.(7oz.) - ground pork
160g.(5³/₅oz.) each - dried turnip, minced celery

120g.(4¼oz.) each -------- squids, oysters
16C. ------------------- stock

1 •75g.(2²/₃oz.) red shallots
•40g.(1²/₅oz.) dried baby shrimp

2 •²/₃t.salt
•½t.pepper

1 Wash squids and cut into serving pieces. Dice dried turnip, soak in water for 10 minutes; drain. Soak dried shrimp in water, drain, and mince. Mince red shallots. Wash oysters, drain.

2 Heat the wok, add 4T. oil and heat; stir fry **1** until fragrant. Add pork and turnip, stir fry until fragrant, remove.

3 Rinse rice, add stock, and bring to a boil over high heat. Then simmer for 15 minutes. Add squids, oysters, and step **2** ingredients. Season with **2** Sprinkle on celery and serve.

香菇竹筍瘦肉粥 • *Mushrooms and Bamboo Congee*

蓬萊米 -------------- ３００公克
熟筍 ----------------- １５０公克
五花肉 -------------- １００公克

香菇 --------------------- １５公克
高湯 ----------------------- １１杯

1｜ 醬油、太白粉、水 --------
　　 --------------------- 各１大匙
　　 酒 ---------------- １小匙
　　 糖、麻油 --------- 各¼小匙

2｜ 胡椒粉 -------------- ２小匙
　　 鹽 ----------------- １½小匙
　　 味精 ----------------- １小匙
　　 麻油 ----------------- ⅛小匙

1 五花肉切絲入 **1** 料醃１０分鐘，香菇泡軟去蒂切絲，筍切絲備用。

2 鍋熱入油３大匙燒熱，入香菇絲及筍絲炒香，再入洗淨之米及高湯，大火煮開，改中火續煮２５分鐘後，續入肉絲煮熟，最後加 **2** 料拌勻即可。

■ 胡椒粉可依個人喜好酌量增減。

■ 米可以７００公克飯取代，煮的時間縮為１５分鐘即可。

300g.(10½oz.) ------- short grain rice
150g.(5⅓oz.) ---- boiled or canned bamboo shoots

100g.(3½oz.) --- pork belly
15g.(½oz.) ----- dried black mushrooms
11C. ------------------- stock

1｜ •1T.each soy sauce, corn starch, water
　　 •1t.cooking wine
　　 •¼t.each sugar, sesame oil

2｜ •2t.pepper
　　 •1½t.salt
　　 •⅛t.sesame oil

1 Shred the pork belly, marinate in **1** for 10 minutes. Soften mushrooms in water, discard the stems, and shred. Shred bamboo shoots.

2 Heat the wok, add 3T. oil and heat; stir fry mushrooms and bamboo shoots until fragrant. Add rinsed rice and stock, bring to a boil over high heat. Then simmer over mediumn heat for 25 minutes, add shredded pork; simmer until cooked. Season with **2**.

■ Amount of pepper depends on personal taste.

■ In order to reduce simmering time to 15 minutes. Rice may be replaced by 700g.(1½lb.) cooked rice.

芋頭瘦肉粥 · *Taro and Pork Congee*

芋頭（淨重）------ 6 0 0公克	瘦肉 ----------------- 2 2 5公克
蓬萊米 ------------- 3 0 0公克	芹菜 ------------------------ 3 0公克

1
- 太白粉、水 ----- 各2大匙
- 麻油 ----------------- 2 小匙
- 鹽、味精 --------- 各½小匙

2
- 鹽 ----------------- 1 ½小匙
- 味精、胡椒粉 --- 各½小匙

1 芋頭去皮與瘦肉均切小丁，肉入 **1** 料拌醃；芹菜切末備用。
2 米洗淨入水 1 6杯及芋頭，大火煮開，改中火煮 1 5分鐘，續入 **2** 料及瘦肉煮熟，起鍋後灑上芹菜即可。

600g.(1⅓lb.) ---- taros (net weight)
300g.(10½oz.) ------- short grain rice

225g.(8oz.) ----- lean pork
30g.(1oz.) ------------ celery

1
- 2T.each corn starch, water
- 2t.sesame oil
- ½t.salt

2
- 1½t.salt
- ½t.pepper

1 Pare taros; dice both taro and pork. Marinate pork in **1**. Mince celery.
2 Rinse rice, add 16C. water and taros, bring to a boil over high heat, simmer over mediumn heat for 15 minutes. Add **2** and pork, simmer until cooked. Sprinkle on celery and serve.

四人份　**serve 4**

雞球粥 · *Chicken Congee*

蓬萊米 ------------- 3 0 0公克	薑絲 --------------------- 1 5公克
雞胸肉 ------------- 2 2 5公克	香菜 ------------------------- 少許

1
- 太白粉、水 --- 各1 ½小匙
- 味精、鹽 --------- 各¼小匙

2
- 鹽 ----------------- ¾小匙
- 胡椒粉、味精 --- 各¼小匙

1 雞胸肉洗淨切小丁，入 **1** 料醃1 0分鐘備用。
2 米洗淨加水1 2杯，大火煮開，改小火煮2 0分鐘，入雞肉續煮 1〜2分鐘後，再入 **2** 料煮開，起鍋後灑上薑絲及香菜即可。

300g.(10½oz.) ------- short grain rice
225g.(8oz.)chicken breast

15g.(½oz.) ------- shredded ginger
dash of ---------- coriander

1
- 1½t.each corn starch, water
- ¼t.salt

2
- ¾t.salt
- ¼t.pepper

1 Wash chicken and dice, marinate in **1** for 10 minutes.
2 Rinse rice and add 12C. water, bring to a boil over high heat; simmer over low heat for 20 minutes. Add chicken then cook for 1-2 minutes, season with **2**; bring to a boil again. Sprinkle on shredded ginger and coriander. Serve.

　四人份　**serve 4**

南瓜甜粥 · *Sweet Pumpkin Congee*

南瓜	450公克	豆沙	25公克
蓬萊米	200公克	糖	7大匙

1 南瓜洗淨去籽切2×2公分塊狀備用。

2 米洗淨入水8杯及南瓜大火煮開，改小火煮20分鐘後，再入豆沙及糖拌勻即可。

450g.(1lb.) -----pumpkins
200g.(7oz.) ---short grain rice

25g.(⁸/₉oz.) ------sweet red bean paste
7T. --------------------sugar

1 Wash pumpkins, discard the seeds, and cut into 2 cm x 2 cm (³/₄" x ³/₄") pieces.

2 Rinse rice, add 8C. water and pumpkin pieces; bring to a boil over high heat. Simmer over low heat for 20 minutes, add sweet red bean paste and sugar, mix well. Serve.

四人份　　serve 4

海鮮粥 · *Seafood Congee*

白飯	700公克		酒	1大匙
蛤蜊	300公克		鹽	1½小匙
花枝	160公克	**1**	味精	1小匙
劍蝦	75公克		胡椒粉	³/₄小匙
香菜、薑絲	各20公克			
高湯	11杯			

1 花枝洗淨切花，劍蝦洗淨用剪刀剪去鬚腳備用。

2 白飯入高湯中煮開，入**1**料調味，煮至稍為濃稠時，再入劍蝦、蛤蜊、花枝及薑絲煮熟，起鍋後灑上香菜即可。

700g.(1½lb.) -cooked rice
300g.(10½oz.) ------clams
160g.(5³/₅oz.) -------squids
75g.(2²/₃oz.) -------shrimp
20g.(²/₃oz.)each coriander, shredded ginger
11C. ------------------stock

1
• 1T.cooking wine
• 1½t.salt
• ³/₄t.pepper

1 Wash squids and cut into serving pieces. Wash shrimp and snip off legs.

2 Bring rice to a boil in stock, season with **1**, simmer until slightly thickened. Add shrimp, clams, squids, and shredded ginger, boil until all cooked. Sprinkle on coriander and serve.

四人份　　serve 4

鮑魚雞絲粥 • *Abalone and Chicken Congee*

蓬萊米 -------------- ３００公克	鮑魚 -------------------- ５０公克
雞胸肉 -------------- １５０公克	薑絲、蔥絲 --------- 各２５公克
熟筍 -------------------- ８０公克	高湯 ---------------------- １１杯

❶ ┌ 蛋白 -------------------- １個
　　 └ 鹽、味精、胡椒粉 --------
　　 　 -------------------- 各¼小匙

❷ ┌ 鮑魚罐頭湯 ----------- １杯
　　 │ 酒 ---------------------- １大匙
　　 │ 鹽 ------------------ １½小匙
　　 │ 味精 ----------------- ½小匙
　　 └ 胡椒粉 --------------- ¼小匙

1 雞胸肉洗淨切絲，入 **❶** 料醃１０分鐘，鮑魚、筍均切絲備用。
2 米洗淨入高湯１１杯，大火煮開，改小火續煮２０分鐘後，入筍絲、薑絲及 **❷** 料煮５分鐘，最後再加入雞絲、鮑魚絲煮熟，並灑上蔥絲即可。

300g.(10½oz.) ------- short grain rice
150g.(5⅓oz.) ------ chicken breast
80g.(2⅘oz.) ----- boiled or canned bamboo shoots

50g.(1¾oz.) ------- canned abalone
25g.(1oz.)each ------------- shredded green onion, shredded ginger
11C. ------------------ stock

❶ ┌ •1 egg white
　　 └ •¼t.each salt, pepper

❷ ┌ •1C.juice of canned abalone
　　 │ •1T.cooking wine
　　 │ •1½t.salt
　　 └ •¼t.pepper

1 Rinse chicken breast and shred, marinate with **❶** for 10 minutes. Shred abalone and bamboo shoots.
2 Rinse rice, add 11C. stock; bring to a boil over high heat. Then simmer over low heat for 20 minutes. Add bamboo shoots, ginger, and **❷**; simmer 5 minutes more. Add chicken and abalone, simmer until cooked. Sprinkle on shredded green onion and serve.

蟹肉粥 • *Crab Congee*

蟹 -------------------- 600公克	薑絲 -------------------- 10公克
蓬萊米 -------------- 200公克	高湯 -------------------- 6杯
蟹肉條 ---------------- 60公克	

1
- 蔥段 -------------------- 4 段
- 薑片 -------------------- 1 片
- 酒 -------------------- 1 大匙

2
- 酒 -------------------- 2 小匙
- 鹽、糖 ----------- 各 1 小匙
- 胡椒粉 --------------⅟₄小匙

1 蟹表面刷乾淨後，揭開殼蓋，將腸泥及鰓去掉並洗淨後，加**1**料入鍋蒸8分鐘，取出待涼，將蟹肉取下備用。

2 蟹肉條撕成細絲備用。

3 米洗淨入高湯及薑絲，大火煮開，改小火煮45分鐘，再入蟹肉、蟹肉條及**2**料煮5分鐘即可。

600g.(1⅓lb.) --------- crabs
200g.(7oz.) --- short grain rice
60g.(2¹/₁₀oz.)imitation crab
10g.(⅓oz.) ------ shredded ginger
6C. -------------------- stock

1
- •4 sections green onion
- •1 slice ginger
- •1T.cooking wine

2
- •2t.cooking wine
- •1t.each salt, sugar
- •¼t.pepper

1 Brush crabs clean, peel off the shells; remove entrails and wash clean. Steam with **1** for 8 minutes, and let cool. Remove all crab meat.

2 Shred imitation carb to fine shreds.

3 Rinse rice, add stock and ginger; bring to boiling; reduce heat and simmer for 45 minutes. Add crab meat, imitation crab, and season with **2**; simmer for 5 minutes.

桂圓糯米粥 • *Sweet Logan Congee*

| 圓糯米 -------------- ３００公克 | 糖 ---------------------------- ½杯 |
| 桂圓肉 -------------- １００公克 | 酒 ------------------------- １大匙 |

1 米洗淨加水１１杯，大火煮開，續入桂圓肉及酒煮開，改小火煮約２０分鐘至米熟爛，再加糖拌勻即可。
■ 粥的甜度可以依個人喜好而增減。

300g.(10½oz.) ------- short grain glutinous rice
100g.(3½oz.) --------- dried logans (pitted)

½C. --------------------- sugar
1T. ----------- cooking wine

1 Rinse rice and add 11C. water, bring to a boil over high heat. Add logans and wine, bring to a boil again; simmer over low heat for 20 minutes until rice tender. Mix sugar in well. Serve.
■ Volume of sugar depends on personal taste.

四人份   **serve 4**

綠豆粥 • *Sweet Green Bean Congee*

| 蓬萊米 -------------- ２００公克 | 綠豆 -------------------------- ½杯 |
| 糖 ----------------------------³/₄杯 | |

1 將綠豆及米分別洗淨，泡水１小時再瀝乾。
2 綠豆加水２杯大火煮開，改小火燜煮１５分鐘，續入７杯水及米大火煮開，改小火續煮２０分鐘，再加入糖拌勻即可。
■ 紅豆粥：將綠豆改成紅豆，燜煮時間再加長。
■ 小米粥：將綠豆改成小米，其餘材料及做法與綠豆粥相同。

200g.(7oz.) ---short grain rice

³/₄C. --------------------- sugar
½C. ----------- mung beans

1 Wash both mung beans and rice. Soak both in water for 1 hour, drain.
2 Add 2C. water in mung beans and bring to a boil, simmer over low heat for 15 minutes. Add 7C. water and rice, bring to a boil over high heat, simmer over low heat for 20 minutes, then add sugar, mix well. Serve.
■ Sweet Red Bean Congee: Replace mung beans with red beans, simmering time should be slightly longer.
■ Sweet Millet Congee: Replace mung beans with millets. The rest remains the same.

四人份   **serve 4**

花生糊 • *Peanuts Porridge*

去皮花生 ----------- ２２５公克　　二砂紅糖 -------------------- ³/₄杯
蓬萊米 ------------- １００公克　　奶水 ------------------------- ¹/₂杯

1 蓬萊米洗淨，瀝乾，以乾鍋小火炒至金黃色。
2 鍋熱入油３杯燒至五分熱（１２０℃），入花生炸至金黃色撈起瀝油備用。
3 將米與花生加水４杯，以果汁機打成花生米漿，另鍋中加水４杯煮開，再倒入花生米漿及糖，邊煮邊攪至沸騰後，續煮３分鐘，熄火，淋上奶水拌勻即可。
4 冷食熱飲皆適宜。

225g.(8oz.) -------- shelled   ³/₄C. ---------- brown sugar
peanuts   ¹/₂C. ------- evaporated milk
100g.(3¹/₂oz.) --------- short
grain rice

1 Wash rice, drain; stir fry in a dry wok over low heat until golden.
2 Heat the wok, add 3C. oil and heat to 120°C (248°F); deep fry peanuts until golden, remove and drain.
3 Add 4C. water into rice and peanuts, puree in a blender to be peanut rice milk. Bring 4C. water to a boil in another pot, pour in peanut rice milk and sugar. Stir constantly until boiled, continue boiling for 3 more minutes, turn off the heat. Mix in the milk and serve.
4 May be served warm or cold.

核桃酪 • *Walnuts Milk*

核桃仁 -------------- ４００公克　　二砂紅糖 -------------------- １杯
在來米 -------------- １００公克　　奶精 ----------------------- １大匙

1 在來米洗淨，泡水３小時，瀝乾後加 ¹/₂ 杯水打成米漿。
2 核桃仁洗淨，泡溫水１小時後瀝乾備用。
3 鍋熱入油３杯燒至六分熱（１４０℃），入核桃仁炸至金黃色取出，加４杯水，以果汁機打成核桃漿備用。
4 核桃漿加５杯水及糖煮開，改小火一面攪拌，一面慢慢倒入米漿，待其煮沸後續煮３分鐘即為核桃酪，食時再淋上奶精即可。

400g.(14oz.) ------ walnuts   1C. ---------- brown sugar
100g.(3¹/₂oz.) --------- long   1T. -------------------- cream
grain rice

1 Wash rice and soak in water for 3 hours; drain. Add ¹/₂C. water and puree in a blender.
2 Wash walnuts, soak in warm water for 1 hour, drain.
3 Heat the wok, add 3C. oil and heat to 140°C (284°F); deep fry walnuts until golden, remove. Add 4C. water and puree in a blender.
4 Bring walnut puree, 5C. water, and sugar to a boil, turn heat to low. Pour in rice puree and constantly stirring the mixture, bring to a boil again; simmer for 3 more minutes. Sprinkle on cream and serve.

三絲腸粉捲 • *Pork Rice Sheet Rolls*

河粉 ----------------- 300公克	熟筍 ---------------------- 45公克
里肌肉、韭黃 ------ 各75公克	香菇 ---------------------- 2公克
金針菇 ----------------- 50公克	

1
- 太白粉、麻油 --- 各½大匙
- 鹽 --------------------- ½小匙
- 味精、糖 -------- 各¼小匙
- 胡椒粉 ----------------- ⅛小匙

2
- 水 ------------------- 1大匙
- 醬油 ----------------- ½大匙
- 麻油、糖 --------- 各½大匙
- 胡椒粉、味精 --- 各⅛小匙

1 里肌肉、筍、香菇均切絲，金針菇去根部，韭黃切段，全部材料與 **1** 料拌勻即為內餡。

2 河粉皮切成10×10公分之正方形（圖1），上置內餡捲成圓筒狀（圖2），淋上 **2** 料，入鍋蒸6分鐘即可。

300g.(10½oz.) --------- flat rice noodle sheets
75g.(2⅔oz.) each ---- pork fillet, yellow chives
50g.(1¾oz.) -------- golden mushrooms

45g.(1⅗oz.) ----- boiled or canned bamboo shoots
2g.(1/14oz.) ------ dried black mushrooms

1
- ½T.each corn starch, sesame oil
- ½t.salt
- ¼t.sugar
- ⅛t.pepper

2
- 1T.water
- ½T.soy sauce
- ½t.each sesame oil, sugar
- ⅛t.pepper

1 Shred pork fillet, bamboo shoots, and mushrooms. Remove the roots of golden mushrooms. Cut yellow chives into serving sections. Mix all materials well with **1** to be the filling.

2 Cut rice noodle sheets into 10 cm x 10 cm (4" x 4") squares (illus. 1), place filling in the center and roll into cylinders (illus. 2). Pour **2** over and steam for 6 minutes.

1

2

牛肉粉捲 • *Beef Rice Sheet Rolls*

河粉 ----------------- ３００公克   牛肉 ----------------- ２００公克

1 ┌ 蔥絲 ------------- ７０公克
      │ 芹菜絲 ----------- ２０公克
      └ 薑絲 ------------- １０公克

2 ┌ 醬油、黑醋、麻油、糖 --
      │ ---------------------各1小匙
      │ 鹽、味精、胡椒粉 --------
      └ ---------------------各½小匙

1 牛肉切細絲，與 **1**、**2** 料拌勻即為內餡。
2 河粉切１０×１０公分之正方形，上置內餡捲成圓筒狀，入鍋大
　　火蒸１０分鐘即可。

300g.(10½oz.) ---- flat rice noodle sheets

200g.(7oz.) ------------ beef

1 ┌ •70g (2½oz) shredded green onion
      │ •20g.(⅔oz.) shredded celery
      └ •10g.(⅓oz.) shredded ginger

2 ┌ •1t.each soy sauce, brown vinegar, sesame oil, sugar
      └ •½t.each salt, pepper

1 Shred beef, and mix well with **1** and **2**. This is the filling.
2 Cut rice noodle sheets into 10 cm x 10 cm (4" x 4") squares, fill with filling and roll into cylinders. Steam over high heat for 10 minutes and serve.

蝦仁河粉捲 • *Shrimp Rice Sheet Rolls*

河粉 ----------------- 3 0 0 公克

1 ┌ 小蝦仁 -------- 1 0 0 公克
　 │ 叉燒肉 ---------- 6 0 公克
　 └ 韭黃 ------------ 4 0 公克

3 太白粉、水 -------- 各½小匙

2 ┌ 白芝麻 ------------- 1 大匙
　 │ 麻油 ----------------- 1 小匙
　 │ 糖 ---------------------- ½小匙
　 │ 鹽 ---------------------- ⅓小匙
　 └ 胡椒粉、味精 --- 各¼小匙

1 叉燒肉切絲，韭黃切段備用。

2 鍋熱入油2大匙燒熱，入 **1** 料炒熟，續入 **2** 料拌勻，再以 **3** 料
　 芶芡即為內餡。

3 河粉皮切成1 0×1 0公分之正方形，上置內餡捲成圓筒狀，入
　 鍋蒸6分鐘即可。

■ 蒸熟河粉捲亦可灑些炒熟的白芝麻。

300g.(10½oz.) ---- flat rice noodle sheets

1 ┌ •100g.(3½oz.) fresh baby shrimp
　 │ •60g.(2⅒oz.) Bar-B-Q pork
　 └ •40g.(1⅖oz.) yellow chives

3 ┌ •½t.each corn starch, water

2 ┌ •1T.white sesame seeds
　 │ •1t.sesame oil
　 │ •½t.sugar
　 │ •⅓t.salt
　 └ •¼t.pepper

1 Shred Bar-B-Q pork. Cut yellow chives into sections.

2 Heat the wok, add 2T. oil and heat; stir fry **1** until cooked. Add **2** and mix well. Thicken with **3** to be the filling.

3 Cut rice noodle sheets into 10 cm x 10 cm (4" x 4") squares, place filling in the center, and roll into cylinders. Steam for 6 minutes and serve.

■ Steamed shrimp rolls may be sprinkled with roasted white sesame seeds before steaming.

干炒牛肉河粉 • *Fried Beef Rice Fettuccini*

河粉 ----------------- 5 2 5公克
牛肉 ----------------- 3 0 0公克
綠豆芽、韭黃 --- 各1 5 0公克

蔥絲 -------------------- 4 0公克
薑片 --------------------- 1 2片

1
醬油、水 ------ 各1⅓大匙
酒 ------------------ 2小匙
糖 ------------------ 1小匙
味精 --------------- ½小匙

2
醬油、水 -------- 各2大匙
太白粉 ----------- 1⅓大匙
麻油、糖 -------- 各2小匙
胡椒粉、味精 --- 各½小匙

1 牛肉洗淨切薄片，入 **1** 料醃1 0分鐘，河粉切1公分寬條，入鍋川燙備用。

2 鍋熱入油2杯燒熱，入牛肉過油至熟撈起，鍋內留油3大匙，爆香薑片、蔥絲，續入綠豆芽、韭黃、河粉及 **2** 料炒勻，最後再倒入牛肉拌炒均勻即可。

525g.(1⅙lb.) ------ flat rice noodle sheets
300g.(10½oz.) -------- beef
150g.(5⅓oz.) each - mung bean sprouts,yellow chives

40g.(1⅖oz.) ----- shredded green onion
12 slices ------------- ginger

1
• 1⅓T.each soy sauce, water
• 2t.cooking wine
• 1t.sugar

2
• 2T.each soy sauce, water
• 1⅓T.corn starch
• 2t.each sesame oil, sugar
• ½t.pepper

1 Rinse beef and slice thin, marinate in **1** for 10 minutes. Cut rice noodle sheets into 1 cm (⅖") wide strips, scald in boiling water.

2 Heat the wok, add 2C. oil and heat; soak beef in hot oil until cooked, lift out. Keep 3T. oil in the wok, stir fry ginger slices and shredded green onion until fragrant; add in bean sprouts, yellow chives, rice strips, and **2**, mix well. Then mix in beef and serve.

芋頭糕 · *Taro Rice Cake*

在來米 -------------- ６００公克	■１	水 ---------------------- ５杯
芋頭（淨重）------ ３００公克		細糖、鹽 -------- 各２小匙
太白粉 ----------------- ７０公克		味精 ---------------- １小匙

1 在來米洗淨，加水浸泡１２小時後，瀝乾，再加３杯水，用果汁機打成米漿，加入太白粉拌勻備用，芋頭刨成絲。

2 鍋熱入油６大匙燒熱，入芋頭絲炒至金黃色，入 ■１ 料煮開，倒入米漿拌勻，再盛起置容器中，入鍋大火蒸１小時即可。

600g.(1⅓lb.) --- long grain rice
300g.(10½oz.) - taros (net weight)
70g.(2½oz.) --- corn starch

■1
- 5C.water
- 2t.each sugar, salt

1 Wash rice, cover with water and soak for 12 hours. Drain, puree in a blender with 3C. water. Mix well with corn starch. Shred taros finely.

2 Add 6T. oil in the wok and heat. Stir fry taros until golden. Season with ■1 bring it to a boil. Pour rice puree into boiling taro soup and mix well. Remove and pour into a container; steam over high heat for 1 hour.

蘿蔔糕 · *Turnip Cake*

在來米 -------------- ６００公克		玻璃紙 ----------------------- １張
■１ 白蘿蔔絲（淨重）-------- ------------- １２００公克	■２	鹽 -------------------- ２小匙
水 ----------------------- １杯		胡椒粉、味精 -- 各１小匙

1 在來米洗淨，泡水１２小時後，瀝乾，加３杯水打成米漿備用。

2 ■１ 料煮２０分鐘至蘿蔔透明且熟爛，隨即加入 ■２ 料及米漿，並開小火，將米漿拌炒至黏稠（約３分鐘），再放入預先舖好玻璃紙之容器內，入鍋大火蒸５０分鐘，以筷子插入不黏時即可。

600g.(1⅓oz.) -- long grain rice   1 sheet - cellophane paper

■1
- 1200g.(2⅗lb.) shredded turnip (net weight)
- 1C.water

■2
- 2t.salt
- 1t.pepper

1 Wash rice, soak in water for 12 hours, and drain. Add 3C. water and puree in a blender.

2 Boil ■1 for 20 minutes until turnips become transparent and tender; pour in ■2 and rice puree. Turn heat to low and stir constantly until thickened (about 3 minutes). Pour the mixture into a cellophane-lined container, steam over high heat for 50 minutes or until a chopstick comes out cleanly.

紅豆糕 · *Ruby Rice Cake*

在來米	300公克	**1**	冰糖	1杯
紅豆	200公克		油	3大匙
玻璃紙	1張			

1 在來米洗淨泡水3小時，瀝乾，再加2杯水打成米漿備用。
2 紅豆加水5杯煮沸，改小火將紅豆煮至熟透但不裂開，再加 **1** 料拌勻熄火，馬上入米漿拌成糊狀。
3 取一蒸盤，舖上玻璃紙，倒入紅豆米漿糊，以大火蒸50分鐘，待涼，直接食用或煎食均可。

300g.(10½oz.)-long grain rice
200g.(7oz.)-----red beans
1 sheet-cellophane paper

1 ┌ •1C.crystal sugar
　　└ •3T.oil

1 Wash rice, soak in water for 3 hours, and drain. Add 2C. water and puree in a blender.
2 Bring 5C. water and red beans to a boil, simmer over low heat until red beans are tender but not yet burst open; mix in **1** well. Turn off the heat and mix with rice puree immediately.
3 Line a steam tray with cellophane paper, pour in red bean-rice mixture. Steam over high heat for 50 minutes, allow to cool. Serve as it is or fried.

發糕 · *Rice Cake with Soda*

1	在來米	600公克	**2** 麵粉	1杯
	水	3杯	泡打粉	4小匙
	糖	2杯		

1 在來米洗淨，以水浸泡12小時後，瀝乾。
2 **1** 料打成米漿，再拌入過篩之 **2** 料拌勻，分別盛於碗內，每碗8分滿，入蒸籠大火蒸30分鐘，以筷子插入不黏即可。

1 ┌ •600g.(1⅓lb.) long grain rice
　　├ •3C.water
　　└ •2C.sugar

2 ┌ •1C.flour
　　└ •4t.baking powder

1 Wash rice and soak in water for 12 hours. Drain.
2 Puree **1** in a blender, mix in sifted **2** well. Place in individual bowls, each about 80% full. Steam in a steamer for 30 minutes. Test with a chopstick, it's done when the chopstick comes out cleanly.

蚵碟 • *Golden Oyster Buns*

韭菜 ----------------- 600公克	■	鹽 ----------------- 2½小匙
在來米 -------------- 300公克		糖 ----------------- 1 小匙
中筋麵粉、生蠔 各200公克		胡椒粉 -------------- ¼小匙

1 在來米洗淨泡水3小時，瀝乾水分，加水至900公克打成米漿後，再入中筋麵粉與 ■ 料拌勻。

2 生蠔加太白粉、鹽拌洗後分成12等份，韭菜洗淨切成1公分段備用。

3 鍋熱入油8杯燒至七分熱（160℃），入湯杓先炸熱，再取出湯杓，淋上2大匙的米漿鋪平（圖1），上加韭菜段25公克，再放1份生蠔（圖2），上面再蓋上25公克韭菜段，最上面再淋上5大匙米漿，即為蚵碟，入油鍋小火炸至凝固，取出湯杓將蚵碟續炸至金黃色且熟透（約5分鐘）即可。

600g.(1⅓lb.) -------- chives	■	•2½t.salt
300g.(10½oz.) -------- long grain rice		•1t.sugar
200g.(7oz.) each -------- all purpose flour, oysters		•¼t.pepper

1 Wash rice and soak in water for 3 hours, drain. Add water into rice up to 900g.(2lb.) and puree in a blender. Mix rice puree with flour and ■ evenly.

2 Rub oysters with corn starch and salt, rinse. Divide oysters into 12 equal portions. Wash chives and cut into 1 cm (²/₅") pieces.

3 Heat the wok, add 8C. oil and heat to 160°C (320°F); heat a soup ladle in the oil. Lift out the ladle and then pour 2T. rice batter into the ladle, spread batter evenly in the ladle (illus. 1), place 25g.(1oz.) chives on top then add a layer of oysters (illus. 2), then another layer of chives, last top with 5T. rice batter. This is the oyster bun. Lower the ladle into wok, deep fry over low heat until the rice batter set. Loosen and carefully remove the buns from the ladle and continue to fry the buns until golden and thoroughly cooked (about 5 minutes). Serve.

1

2

碗粿 • *Pork Wa Guey*

在來米 -------------- 400公克	紅蔥頭 ------------------ 10公克
絞肉 ----------------- 150公克	香菇 ----------------------- 4公克
蘿蔔乾 ----------------- 75公克	鹹蛋黃 ----------------------- 4個

1「 水 --------------------- 6杯
  鹽、胡椒粉 ------ 各½小匙

2「 醬油 ----------------- 2小匙
  味精 ----------------- ¼小匙

1 紅蔥頭切薄片，蘿蔔乾剁碎並泡水至不鹹再瀝乾，香菇泡軟去蒂，與鹹蛋黃各切成兩半備用。
2 鍋熱入油4大匙燒熱，將紅蔥頭炒香，續入絞肉、香菇和蘿蔔乾炒熟，再入 **1** 料炒勻備用。
3 在來米洗淨，以適量的水浸泡12小時，瀝乾，再加 **2** 料打成米漿後，入鍋隔水加熱煮至黏稠（圖1），煮時需不斷攪動，將米漿分盛在8個碗內，每碗8分滿（圖2），再將炒香之肉餡及鹹蛋黃置於其上，入鍋大火蒸30分鐘即可。

400g.(14oz.)---long grain rice
150g.(5⅓oz.) ground pork
75g.(2⅔oz.)-- dried turnip
10g.(⅓oz.) ---- red shallots

4g.(⅟₇oz.) ------ dried black mushrooms
4 ------- salt-preserved egg yolks

1 •6C.water
  •½t.each salt, pepper

2 •2t.soy sauce

1 Cut shallots into thin slices, chop turnip finely and soak in cold water until unsalty, drain. Soften mushrooms in warm water then discard stems. Halve mushrooms and egg yolks.
2 Heat the wok, add 4T. oil, stir fry shallots until fragrant. Add pork, mushrooms and turnip, stir fry until all are cooked, then add **1**, mix evenly. This is the filling.
3 Wash rice and cover with cold water, soak for 12 hours. Drain and puree in a blender with **2**. Simmer over low heat until thickened (illus. 1), stir constantly during cooking. Pour thicken rice puree into 8 bowls, until each about 80% full (illus. 2); fill each center with filling and a egg yolk on top. Steam over high heat for 30 minutes. Serve.

1

2

甜碗粿 • *Sweet Wa Guey*

| 在來米 -------------- ４００公克 | **1** | 水 --------------------- 6杯 |
| | | 紅糖 ------------------- 1杯 |

1 在來米洗淨以適量的水浸泡１２小時，瀝乾再加 **1** 料打成米漿後，以小火煮至黏稠，煮時需不斷攪動。
2 米漿分盛在８個碗內，每碗８分滿，入鍋大火蒸３０分鐘即可。

| 400g.(14oz.) ----------long grain rice | **1** | •6C.water
•1C.dark brown sugar |

1 Wash rice and soak in water for 12 hours, drain. Add in **1** and puree in a blender. Boil rice puree over low heat until thickened, stir constantly.
2 Pour thickened rice puree into 8 individual bowls, each about 80% full. Steam over high heat for 30 minutes.

米奶 • *Rice Milk*

| 蓬萊米 -------------- １００公克 | 花生 -------------------- ２５公克 |
| 細糖 ------------------------- 1杯 | |

1 花生入乾鍋用小火炒至熟且深褐色，蓬萊米泡水１２小時後瀝乾。
2 所有材料加１杯水打成米漿，備用。
3 水１０杯煮沸，加入米漿，煮滾即可。

| 100g.(3½oz.) -short grain rice | 1C. --------------------sugar |
| | 25g.(1oz.) --------peanuts |

1 Stir fry peanuts in a dry wok over low heat. Then cook until done, when they will be a dark brown color. Soak rice in water for 12 hours. Drain.
2 Puree all the ingredients with 1C. water in a blender.
3 Bring 10C. water to a boil, add in rice porridge, and bring to a boil again.

芝麻糯米球 · *Sesame Seeds Rice Balls*

豆沙 ----------------- 300公克	澄粉 --------------------- 50公克	
糯米粉 -------------- 200公克	細糖 --------------------------- 1/3杯	
白芝麻 -------------- 100公克		

1 澄粉過篩加開水 1/4 杯調成糊狀，續入糯米粉、糖拌揉均勻後，再慢慢加冷水揉成麵糰，分成20等份即為麵皮。

2 豆沙分成20等份備用。

3 每份麵皮包入豆沙搓成湯圓狀，沾濕後再沾芝麻備用。

4 油4杯燒至三分熱（70～80℃），入芝麻球小火慢炸至浮起，再開大火並輕壓芝麻球，使之膨起成金黃色即可。

300g.(10½oz.) -sweet red bean paste
200g.(7oz.) -----glutinous rice flour
100g.(3½oz.) ------- white sesame seeds
50g.(1¾oz.) wheat starch
1/3C. --------------------sugar

1 Sift wheat starch and mix with boiling water to a paste; then add rice flour and sugar, mix well. Add cold water slowly and knead into dough, divide into 20 equal portions.

2 Divide sweet red bean paste equally into 20 portions.

3 Use red bean paste as filling, place each filling into the center of a dough; roll into balls. Dampen the surface and roll on some sesame seeds.

4 Heat the wok, add 4C. oil; heat to 70 - 80°C (140 - 160°F), deep fry sesame seeds balls slowly until floating. Turn heat to high, gently press on sesame seeds balls, then they will swell up like a balloon and turn golden. Lift out, drain and serve.

酒釀湯圓 · *Sweet Wine Rice Dough Balls*

罐頭桔子 ----------------- 10片	**1**⌈ 小湯圓 -------- 150公克	
蛋 --------------------------- 1個	└ 細糖 ---------------- 6大匙	
酒釀 -------------------------- 3大匙		
桂花醬 ----------------------- 1/4小匙		

1 水4杯煮開，入 **1** 料大火煮至湯圓浮起，再加桔子續煮1分鐘後，倒入打散之蛋液、酒釀，熄火，加桂花醬拌勻即可。

10 slices ------------canned tangerines
1 ------------------------egg
3T. --fermented wine rice
1/4t. sweet osmanthus jam

1⌈ •150g.(5⅓oz.) small sweet rice dough balls
└ •6T.sugar

1 Bring 4C. water to a boil, add **1**, boil until rice balls float on top. Add tangerines, boil for 1 minute, stir in beaten egg and fermented wine rice; turn off the heat. Mix in sweet osmanthus jam. Serve.

鹹湯圓 • *Shallot Rice Balls*

圓糯米 -------------- 3 0 0公克		
茼蒿 ------------------ 1 0 0公克		
紅蔥頭 ------------------ 1 0公克		
蝦米 ---------------------- 5公克		
食用紅色 5 號 -------------- 少許		

❶
```
水 ----------------------- 6 杯
鹽 --------------------- ½小匙
味精 ------------------- ¼小匙
```

1 圓糯米製成粿粉糰,再加水 ¼ 杯揉勻至不會乾裂(圖 1),將其分為兩半,一半加紅色素並揉勻,兩者再分別搓揉成圓長條,再分切成 5 公克之小粿糰(圖 2),放置兩掌中間搓成小圓球(圖 3)即為湯圓。
2 紅蔥頭洗淨切片,蝦米洗淨切末,茼蒿洗淨備用。
3 鍋熱入油 3 大匙燒熱,爆香紅蔥頭及蝦米,再入 ❶ 料煮開後,續入湯圓煮至浮起,再放入茼蒿煮開即可。

300g.(10½oz.) ------- short grain glutinous rice
100g.(3½oz.) ------- crown daisy
10g.(⅓oz.) ---- red shallots
5g.(⅕oz.) ------- dried baby shrimp
dash of red food coloring

❶
- 6C. water
- ½t. salt

1 Make glutinous rice into rice flour dough: add ¼C. water and knead to prevent cracking (illus. 1). Divide into 2 equal portions; add red coloring into one portion. Knead both doughs into two long strips, then cut into 5g.(⅕oz.) small pieces (illus. 2). Roll the dough pieces between the palms into small balls (illus. 3).
2 Wash and slice shallots. Wash and mince dried baby shrimp. Wash crown daisy.
3 Heat the wok, add 3T. oil and heat; stir fry shallots and shrimp until fragrant. Add ❶ and bring to a boil; add rice balls, boil until rice balls are all floating on top. Add crown daisy, bring to a boil and serve.

1

2

3

炸元宵 • *Fried Yuan Hsiao*

糯米粉 -------------- ２００公克
熱開水 ------------------------ ½杯

1
糖粉 -------------- 3⅓大匙
黑芝麻粉 --------- 2⅔大匙
豬油 -------------- 2⅓大匙
雪白油 ------------- 1大匙

1 糯米粉圍成粉牆，加入 ½ 杯熱開水，拌勻成粉糰後分成１２等份即為外皮，備用。

2 **1** 料拌勻，放入冰箱中冷凍後，分成１２等份即為內餡，備用。

3 取 1 份外皮包入 1 份內餡，入六分熱（１４０℃）油鍋炸成金黃色即可。

■ 元宵炸好起鍋時，會產生爆裂，小心內餡飛濺。

200g.(7oz.) ----- glutinous rice flour
½C. -------------- hot water

1
- 3⅓T. powdered sugar
- 2⅔T. black sesame powder
- 2⅓T. lard
- 1T. shortening

1 Build a wall with rice flour on a working table, add ½C. hot water; mix well to dough. Divide into 12 equal portions. These are the wrappers.

2 Mix **1** well, freeze in freezer until hard; divide into 12 equal portion fillings.

3 Wrap each filling with one wrapper and roll into a ball. Deep fry in 140°C (284°F) oil until golden.

■ Beware that yuan hsiao may burst open when removed from oil.

椰絲糯米球 • *Coconut Rice Dough Balls*

| 紅豆沙 -------------- 2 4 0 公克 | 櫻桃 ------------------------- 1 個 |
| 椰子粉 ----------------- 6 0 公克 | |

1⎡ 糯米粉 -------- 2 2 0 公克
 ⎣ 澄粉 ----------- 4 0 公克

2⎡ 細糖 -------------- 2 ½ 大匙
 ⎣ 豬油、水 -------- 各 2 大匙

1 紅豆沙分成 2 4 等份，並搓成圓球狀備用。
2 **1**料過篩，入 **2**料拌勻，再入 ¾ 杯開水燙勻（圖 1）並揉成長條狀，分成 2 4 等份，即為粿粉皮。
3 取粿粉皮包 1 份豆沙餡（圖 2），揉圓即為糯米球。
4 一鍋水煮開，入糯米球煮 5 分鐘，見膨脹且浮起後撈起，趁熱放入椰子粉中沾裹均勻排盤，再飾以切碎的櫻桃即可。

240g.(8²/₅oz.) --sweet red bean paste

60g.(2¹/₁₀oz.) ---desiccated coconut

1 -----------------------cherry

1⎡ •220g.(7³/₄oz.) glutinous rice flour
 ⎣ •40g.(1²/₅oz.) wheat starch

2⎡ •2½T.sugar
 ⎣ •2T.each lard, water

1 Divide red bean paste into 24 equal portions, roll into balls.
2 Sift **1**, mix in **2** evenly; add ¾C. hot water (illus. 1), and knead into a long strip. Divide the dough into 24 equal portions to be the rice flour wrappers.
3 Wrap each red bean paste filling into one wrapper (illus. 2), roll into rice balls.
4 Bring a pot of water to a boil, drop rice balls into the boiling water and boil for 5 minutes; lift out when swelling up and floating on top. While warm, roll the rice balls in desiccated coconut. Arrange the rice balls on a plate, decorate with chopped cherry and serve.

1

2

軟脆豆沙捲 • *Crispy Red Bean Rolls*

紅心地瓜 ----------- 6 0 0 公克	**1** ⎡ 糯米粉 -------- 2 0 0 公克
豆沙 ---------------- 2 0 0 公克	⎣ 細糖 --------------- 2 大匙
白芝麻 -------------- 1 0 0 公克	

1 將豆沙分成 2 0 等份備用。
2 紅心地瓜去皮洗淨切丁，入蒸籠蒸 2 0 分鐘，取出趁熱搗爛並加入 **1** 料揉勻，再搓成長條狀（圖 1），分成 2 0 個小粿糰（圖 2 ）。
3 每個小粿糰中間包入豆沙（圖 3 ），收口捏緊，再搓成長圓條，沾水滾上白芝麻即為豆沙捲。
4 鍋熱入油 8 杯燒至六分熱（ 1 4 0 ℃），入豆沙捲，用中火炸至金黃色即可。

600g.(1⅓lb.) ---- red yams	**1** ⎡ •200g.(7oz.)glutinous
200g.(7oz.) ----- sweet red	rice flour
bean paste	•2T.sugar
100g.(3½oz.) -------- white	
sesame seeds	

1 Divide sweet red bean paste into 20 equal portions.
2 Pare yams, wash and dice; steam for 20 minutes, mash while still warm, mix well with **1** and knead to a long strip (illus. 1), divide into 20 small dough balls (illus. 2).
3 Wrap each red bean paste filling with one dough ball (illus. 3), tightly seal the openings, and knead to make long rolls. Sprinkle on some water then roll in the sesame seeds.
4 Heat the wok, add 8C. oil and heat to 140°C (284°F); deep fry rolls over medium heat until golden.

1

2

3

73

粿粽

•Guey Dumplings

鹹水餃 • *Fried Pork Dumplings*

1
絞肉	150公克
熟筍	90公克
蝦米	20公克
香菇	12公克
紅蔥頭末	3大匙

2
糯米粉	300公克
太白粉	100公克
開水	1½杯
糖、油	各2大匙

3
水	½杯
麻油	2小匙
酒、糖	各1小匙
鹽	⅔小匙
胡椒粉	¼小匙

4
水	1大匙
太白粉	1小匙

1 香菇泡軟去蒂，與筍、蝦米均切小丁，鍋熱入油3大匙燒熱，入 **1** 料炒熟並加 **3** 料調味後，以 **4** 料芶芡，即為內餡，待涼備用。

2 **2** 料揉勻至光滑後，搓成長條狀，分成20等份，每份壓成圓薄狀（圖1），內餡置其中（圖2），再把餃皮對折捏合（圖3），即為鹹水餃，若黏手時，則手可沾些沙拉油。

3 鍋熱入油6杯燒至七分熱（160℃），將鹹水餃入鍋中火炸至微硬（約10分鐘），再開大火炸至金黃色即可。

1
- 150g.(5⅓oz.) ground pork
- 90g.(3⅕oz.) boiled or canned bamboo shoots
- 20g.(⅔oz.) dried baby shrimp
- 12g.(⅖oz.) dried black mushrooms
- 3T.minced red shallot

2
- 300g.(10½oz.) glutinous rice flour
- 100g.(3½oz.) corn starch
- 1½C.hot water
- 2T.each sugar, oil

3
- ½C.water
- 2t.sesame oil
- 1t.each cooking wine, sugar
- ⅔t.salt
- ¼t.pepper

4
- 1T.water
- 1t.corn starch

1 Soften dried black mushrooms in water, discard the stems; dice with bamboo shoots and dried shrimp. Heat the wok, add 3t. oil and heat; stir fry **1** until cooked, season with **3**. Thicken with **4**. This is the filling, allow it to cool.

2 Mix and knead **2** until smooth, roll into a long strip; divide into 20 equal portions. Press each into a round thin wrapper (illus. 1). Place a filling in the center (illus. 2), fold it to half (illus. 3). Wet palms with some salad oil to prevent sticking.

3 Heat the wok, add 6C. oil and heat to 160℃ (320°F); deep fry dumplings over medium heat until slightly hardened (about 10 minutes). Then turn the heat to high and fry until golden.

1

2

3

南瓜糕

•Pumpkin Rice Cake

南瓜糕 • *Pumpkin Rice Cake*

	南瓜	600公克
	葡萄乾	30公克

❶
- 糯米粉 -------- 200公克
- 麵粉 ------------ 50公克
- 細糖 ------------ 2大匙
- 豬油 ------------ 1小匙

❷
- 絞肉 ---------- 150公克
- 蘿蔔乾 --------- 75公克
- 紅蔥頭 --------- 25公克
- 蝦米 ------------ 10公克
- 香菇 ------------- 5公克

❸
- 醬油 ----------------- 1大匙
- 鹽、糖、酒 ----- 各1小匙
- 胡椒粉 ----------------¼小匙

1 南瓜切開去籽入鍋蒸20分鐘至熟，取出刮下南瓜肉並瀝乾水分，趁熱倒入盆中與 ❶ 料拌勻為南瓜粿糰，均分成30等份備用。

2 蘿蔔乾、紅蔥頭洗淨切小丁，香菇、蝦米泡軟洗淨亦切小丁備用。

3 鍋熱入油3大匙燒熱，將 ❷ 料爆香，再入 ❸ 料炒勻，待涼即為內餡。

4 每份南瓜粿糰，中間填入內餡10公克（圖1），收口包住揉圓（若黏手可沾少許麵粉），再用麵刀從正面劃4刀（圖2），中間壓入1顆葡萄乾（圖3），排入蒸籠大火蒸7分鐘即可。

600g.(1⅓lb.)	pumpkins
30g.(1oz.)	raisins

❶
- 200g.(7oz.) glutinous rice flour
- 50g.(1¾oz.) flour
- 2T.sugar
- 1t.lard

❷
- 150g.(5⅓oz.) ground pork
- 75g.(2⅔oz.) dried turnip
- 25g.(⁸⁄₉oz.) red shallots
- 10g.(⅓oz.) dried baby shrimp
- 5g.(⅕oz.) dried black mushrooms

❸
- 1T.soy sauce
- 1t.each salt, sugar, cooking wine
- ¼t.pepper

1 Cut pumpkins open, remove all seeds, steam for 20 minutes; scrape off all meat and drain. While still warm, mix pumpkins with **❶**. This is the pumpkin rice dough. Divide into 30 equal portions.

2 Wash dried turnip and red shallots, dice. Soften dried mushrooms and dried shrimp in water, drain, and dice both.

3 Heat the wok, add 3T. oil and heat; stir fry **❷** until fragrant. Add **❸**, stir fry and mix well, allow to cool. This is the filling.

4 Wrap each filling (10g. or ⅓oz.) with a portion of dough (illus. 1), seal the opening and roll to a ball (dust palms with flour to prevent sticking). Score a cross on the surface (illus. 2), press a raisin in the center (illus. 3). Steam over high heat for 7 minutes. Serve.

1

2

3

炒寧波年糕 • *Fried Nin Po Rice Cakes*

寧波年糕 ---------- 6 0 0公克	醬油 ---------------- 1 小匙
大白菜 ------------- 3 0 0公克	

1
| 里肌肉 ----------- 7 5公克 |
| 香菇、蝦米 --各 1 0公克 |

2
| 水 ------------------- 1 杯 |
| 鹽 ------------------- 1 小匙 |
| 味精 ----------------- ½小匙 |

1 里肌肉切絲加醬油醃 1 0分鐘。

2 寧波年糕斜切 0．2公分厚的薄片，香菇泡軟去蒂洗淨切絲，大白菜洗淨切大塊，蝦米泡軟切小丁備用。

3 鍋熱入油 3 大匙燒熱，入 **1** 料爆炒均勻，再入大白菜、寧波年糕及 **2** 料炒勻並煮開，蓋鍋蓋燜煮 2 分鐘即可。

600g.(1⅓lb.) -- Nin Po rice cakes

300g.(10½oz.) ---Chinese cabbage

1t. ---------------soy sauce

1
- •75g.(2⅔oz.) pork fillet
- •10g.(⅓oz.)each dried black mushrooms, dried baby shrimp

2
- •1C.water
- •1t.salt

1 Shred pork and marinate with soy sauce for 10 minutes.

2 Cut rice cakes into slanting 0.2 cm (1/12") thin slices. Soften dried black mushrooms in water, discard the stems, and shred. Wash cabbage and cut into large pieces. Soften dried shrimp in water and dice.

3 Heat the wok, add 3T. oil and heat; stir fry **1** until well-mixed. Add the cabbage, rice cakes, and **2**, mix well and bring to boiling; cover with lid and simmer for 2 minutes.

三絲炒米苔目 • *Fried Pork Mi Tai Ma*

米苔目 -------------- 400公克		紅蔥頭 ---------------- 30公克	
熟筍 ---------------- 220公克		香菇 ------------------ 10公克	
里肌肉 -------------- 150公克		芹菜末 -------------------- 3大匙	

1「 醬油 ----------------- 1大匙
　　太白粉、水 ----- 各1小匙

2「 鹽、味精、糖 --- 各½小匙
　　胡椒粉 -------------- ¼小匙

1 米苔目入開水中川燙，撈起瀝乾水分備用。

2 里肌肉切絲入 **1** 料醃10分鐘，香菇泡軟去蒂後與筍均切絲，紅蔥頭切片備用。

3 鍋熱入油4大匙燒熱，先入肉絲炒至熟取出，再入紅蔥頭炒至金黃色後，續入筍、香菇炒香，最後再入米苔目、肉絲及 **2** 料拌勻，起鍋前再灑上芹菜末即可。

400g.(14oz.) --- Mi Tai Ma
220g.(7¾oz.) --- boiled or canned bamboo shoots
150g.(5⅓oz.) --- pork fillet

30g.(1oz.) ---- red shallots
10g.(⅓oz.) ----- dried black mushrooms
3T. ---------- minced celery

1「 • 1T.soy sauce
　　• 1t.each corn starch, water

2「 • ½t.each salt, sugar
　　• ¼t.pepper

1 Scald Mi Tai Ma in boiling water, drain.

2 Shred pork fillet and marinate in **1** for 10 minutes. Soften dried black mushrooms in water, discard the stems and shred. Shred bamboo shoots. Slice red shallots.

3 Heat the wok, add 4T. oil and heat; stir fry pork until cooked, remove. Stir fry shallots until golden, add bamboo shoots and mushrooms, stir fry until fragrant. Then add the Mi Tai Ma, pork, and **2**; mix well. Sprinkle on minced celery and serve.

米粉羹

• Rice Noodles Pottage

四人份　　**serve 4**

米粉羹　*Rice Noodles Pottage*

熟米粉	1000公克
魚漿	300公克
里肌肉	100公克
高湯	8杯
柴魚片	3大匙
太白粉	1大匙
紅蔥頭片	1/2大匙
麻油	1/2小匙
香菜	少許

1
- 熟筍 ------- 100公克
- 胡蘿蔔 ----- 75公克
- 香菇 ------- 2公克

2
- 醬油、太白粉 --各1小匙
- 鹽 ----- 1/4小匙
- 味精 ----- 1/8小匙

3
- 醬油、黑醋 ----- 各2大匙
- 鹽 ----- 1小匙
- 味精、胡椒粉 --- 各1/2小匙

4
- 水 ----- 8大匙
- 太白粉 ----- 4大匙

1 肉切成0.5公分之條狀，入**2**料醃20分鐘。
2 魚漿加太白粉攪拌後（圖1），肉沾魚漿（圖2）入沸水煮至浮起撈出（圖3）即為肉羹。
3 香菇泡軟去蒂切絲，胡蘿蔔煮熟與筍均切絲。
4 鍋熱入油1/4杯燒熱，爆香紅蔥頭後，入高湯煮開，再入肉羹及**1**料煮開後，續煮片刻，最後再入柴魚片、**3**料調味，並以**4**料芶芡即為肉羹湯。
5 熟米粉置於碗中，入肉羹湯再灑上香菜、麻油即可。

1000g.(2⅕oz.)	boiled rice noodles
300g.(10½oz.)	fish paste (surimi)
100g.(3½oz.)	pork fillet
8C.	stock
3T.	wood fish flake
1T.	corn starch
½T.	red shallots
½t.	sesame oil
dash of	coriander

1
- 100g.(3½oz.) boiled or canned bamboo shoots
- 75g.(2⅔oz.) carrots
- 2g.(1/10oz.) dried black mushrooms

2
- 1t.each soy sauce, corn starch
- ¼t.salt

3
- 2T.each soy sauce, brown vinegar
- 1t.salt
- ½t.pepper

4
- 8T.water
- 4T.corn starch

1 Cut pork into 0.5 cm (¼") strips and marinate with **2** for 20 minutes.
2 Mix fish paste with corn starch (illus. 1); dip pork in the mixture (illus. 2). Add pork into boiling water until floating (illus. 3). Lift out.
3 Soften mushrooms in warm water, discard the stems; shred. Boil bamboo shoots and carrots, drain and shred.
4 Heat the wok, add ¼C. oil; stir fry shallots. Add the stock, then the pork and **1**; bring to boiling again and simmer for a while. Add wood fish flake, season with **3** then thicken with **4**. This is the pork pottage.
5 Place boiled rice noodles in a bowl, pour over pork pottage. Sprinkle on coriander and sesame oil. Serve.

1

2

3

擔擔米粉

•*Dan Dan Rice Noodles*

四人份　**serve 4**

擔擔米粉 • *Dan Dan Rice Noodles*

絞肉 ----------------- 350公克	350g.(12⅓oz.) --------------------------- ground pork
濕米粉（細）------ 300公克	300g.(10½oz.) --------------------- wet rice noodles (thin)
綠豆芽 ------------- 240公克	240g.(8⅖oz.) ------------------------ mung bean sprouts
韭菜 ------------------- 80公克	80g.(2⅘oz.) --- chives
高湯 ---------------------- 8杯	8C. -- stock
紅蔥頭末 ------------- 6大匙	6T. --------------------------------------- minced red shallot
蒜末 ---------------------- 1大匙	1T. -- minced garlic

1
- 高湯 ------------------ 1杯
- 醬油、甜麵醬 各1½大匙
- 酒 ------------------------ 1大匙
- 糖 ------------------------ 1小匙
- 胡椒粉、味精 --- 各½小匙
- 鹽、五香粉 ------ 各¼小匙

1
- 1C.stock
- 1½T.each soy sauce, sweet soy bean paste
- 1T.cooking wine
- 1t.sugar
- ¼t.each salt, five spices powder

2
- 鹽、麻油 -------- 各1小匙
- 味精 ---------------- ¼小匙
- 胡椒粉 -------------- ⅛小匙

2
- 1t.each salt, sesame oil
- ⅛t.pepper

1 鍋熱入油3大匙燒熱，入紅蔥頭、蒜頭爆香，續入絞肉炒熟後，再入 **1** 料拌炒均勻，並以小火燜煮約30分鐘，其間每隔10分鐘翻攪一次，煮好即為肉燥。

2 另鍋中入高湯及 **2** 料煮開，即為米粉湯。

3 米粉分四次入竹漏杓內（圖1），入滾開水中抖動（圖2）至米粉熟軟後，扣入碗中（圖3），韭菜、綠豆芽以同樣方式燙熟後置於米粉上，淋上肉燥並加上米粉湯即可。

1 Heat the wok, add 3T. oil and heat; stir fry minced shallot and minced garlic until fragrant. Add pork, stir fry until cooked. Mix in **1** evenly, simmer for 30 minutes, stir every 10 minutes. This is the meat sauce.

2 In a pot, bring stock and **2** to boiling. This is the soup.

3 Divide rice noodles into 4 bamboo strainers (illus. 1), lower into boiling water and shake constantly (illus. 2), boil until rice noodles softened; invert into individual bowls (illus. 3). Boil chives and mung bean sprouts with the same method and arrange them on top of the rice noodles. Pour meat sauce and then soup over all.

1

2

3

海鲜米粉

•Seafood Rice Noodles

四人份　serve 4

海鮮米粉 • *Seafood Rice Noodles*

熟米粉 ----------- 1000公克
花枝 -------------- 300公克
芹菜、海參 ------ 各150公克
瘦肉、熟洋菇 ------ 各60公克
高湯 -------------- 8杯
劍蝦 -------------- 12隻
蔥段 -------------- 5段

1
  - 水 ---------------- 1杯
  - 酒 ----------------- ½大匙
  - 薑片 -------------- 1片

2
  - 太白粉 ------------ ¼小匙
  - 鹽、胡椒粉 ------ 各⅛小匙

3
  - 醬油 -------------- 1大匙
  - 酒、麻油 ------ 各1½小匙
  - 鹽 --------------- 1小匙
  - 味精、黑醋 ------ 各½小匙
  - 胡椒粉 ------------ ⅛小匙

1 海參去腸泥洗淨切滾刀塊，入 **1** 料川燙撈起洗淨，花枝洗淨切花刀條狀，熟洋菇洗淨切片，芹菜去葉切段。
2 瘦肉切絲入 **2** 料醃30分鐘，鍋熱入油4杯燒至六分熱（140℃），入肉絲及花枝過油撈起。
3 鍋中留油2大匙，入蔥段、洋菇、劍蝦拌炒一下，續入高湯煮開，以 **3** 料調味，再入花枝、海參、肉絲和芹菜煮開，即為海鮮湯，最後入熟米粉即可。

1000g.(2⅕lb.) --------------------------- boiled rice noodles
300g.(10½oz.) --- squids
150g.(5⅓oz.) each -------------------- celery, sea cucumber
60g.(2¹/₁₀oz.) each lean pork,boiled buttton mushrooms
8C. --- stock
12 -- shrimp
5 sections -- green onion

1
  - 1C.water
  - ½T.cooking wine
  - 1 slice ginger

2
  - ¼t.corn starch
  - ⅛t.each salt, pepper

3
  - 1T.soy sauce
  - 1½t.each cooking wine, sesame oil
  - 1t.salt
  - ½t.brown vinegar
  - ⅛t.pepper

1 Remove entrails and wash sea cucumber, cut into serving pieces, parboil with **1** in boiling water; drain and wash. Wash squids and cut into strips. Rinse buttom mushrooms and slice. Remove leaves on celery and cut into sections.
2 Shred pork and marinate in **2** for 30 minutes. Heat the wok, add 4C. oil and heat to 140°C (280°F); dip pork and squids in oil, remove immediately.
3 Keep 2T. oil in the wok, stir fry green onion sections, button mushrooms, and shrimp; add stock and bring to a boil, season with **3**. Add the squids, sea cucumber, pork, and celery; bring to boiling. Then add rice noodles.

酸辣米粉

• *Sour and Spicy Rice Noodles*

四人份　**serve 4**

酸辣米粉 •*Sour and Spicy Rice Noodles*

熟米粉（粗） --- 1000公克	1000g.(2⅕lb.) ------------------- boiled rice noodles (thick)
豆腐 ----------------- 220公克	220g.(7¾oz.) --------------------------------- bean curd
雞血 ----------------- 200公克	200g.(7oz.) -------------------------------- chicken blood
里肌肉 -------------- 150公克	150g.(5⅓oz.) --------------------------------- pork fillet
胡蘿蔔 -------------- 120公克	120g.(4⅓oz.) ------------------------------------- carrots
濕木耳 -------------- 100公克	100g.(3½oz.) ------------------- soaked black wood ears
高湯 ------------------- 8杯	8C. --- stock
蛋 --------------------- 2個	2 --- eggs
蔥末 ------------------ 2½大匙	2½T. ------------------------------- minced green onion

1 醬油、太白粉 -- 各2小匙
　　麻油 --------------- 1小匙

2 白醋 -------------- 3大匙
　　醬油 -------------- 2大匙
　　麻油 -------------- 1大匙
　　糖 --------------- 2小匙
　　鹽、胡椒粉 ----- 各1小匙
　　味精 --------------- ½小匙

3 水 --------------- 2大匙
　　太白粉 ------------- 1大匙

1 •2t.each soy sauce, corn starch
•1t.sesame oil

2 •3T.white vinegar
•2T.soy sauce
•1T.sesame oil
•2t.sugar
•1t.each salt, pepper

3 •2T.water
•1T.corn starch

1 豆腐、雞血、木耳均切絲，胡蘿蔔去皮洗淨切細絲，里肌肉切細絲後入 **1** 料醃5分鐘備用。

2 高湯煮開入豆腐、雞血、木耳及胡蘿蔔煮開後，入 **2** 料煮5分鐘，再入米粉、肉絲煮5分鐘，以 **3** 料芶芡，再入打散之蛋液煮開起鍋後，再灑上蔥末即可。

■ 如無雞血可以豬血代替。

1 Shred bean curd, chicken blood, and wood ears. Pare carrots, wash and shred. Shred pork and marinate in **1** for 5 minutes.

2 Boil the stock, add the bean curd, chicken blood, wood ears, and carrots; bring to a boil again. Add **2** boil for 5 minutes, then add rice noodles and pork, boil for 5 more minutes, thicken with **3**. Stir in beaten eggs, bring to a boil. Sprinkle on minced green onion and serve.

■ Pig blood may be used instead of chicken blood.

星洲炒米粉 • *Singaporean Fried Rice Noodles*

乾米粉（細）------ 300公克		洋蔥 ---------- 200公克	
蝦米 -------------------- 30公克	**1**	熟筍 ----------- 70公克	**1**
高湯 ------------------------ 2杯		胡蘿蔔 ---------- 60公克	
		咖哩粉 -------------- 1大匙	
叉燒肉、西洋芹 -----------		鹽 --------------------- ³/₄小匙	**3**
2 ------------ 各100公克	**2**	味精 ----------------- ¹/₂小匙	

1 米粉泡軟，蝦米洗淨，**1**、**2** 料均切絲備用。
2 鍋熱入油4大匙燒熱，入蝦米爆香，續入 **1** 料炒軟，以 **3** 料調味，再入 **2** 料炒熟，並入高湯煮開後，入米粉拌炒至湯汁收乾即可。

300g.(10¹/₂oz.) -- dried rice noodles

1
- •200g.(7oz.) onion
- •70g.(2¹/₂oz.) boiled or canned bamboo shoots
- •60g.(2¹/₁₀oz.) carrots

2
- •100g.(3¹/₂oz.) each Bar-B-Q pork, celery

30g.(1oz.) ----- dried baby shrimp
2C. --------------------- stock

3
- •1T.curry powder
- •³/₄t.salt

1 Soak the rice noodles in water until softened. Wash dried baby shrimp. Shred both **1** and **2** ingredients.
2 Heat the wok, add 4T. oil and heat; stir fry shrimp until fragrant. Add **1** to fry until all softened. Season with **3**, add **2** to fry until cooked. Pour in stock and bring to a boil. Stir in rice noodles, stir fry until all soup dried out. Serve.

南瓜炒米粉 • *Pumpkin Fried Rice Noodles*

蛤蜊 ------------------ ６００公克　　乾米粉（細）------ ３００公克
南瓜 ------------------ ５８０公克

1
　蔥段 ------------------ １２段
　蝦米 ------------------ ２０公克
　香菇 ------------------ ５公克

2
　水 ---------------------- １杯
　鹽 ------------------ １¼小匙
　味精、黑胡椒粉 各¼小匙

1 南瓜去皮、籽洗淨切絲；鍋內入水燒開後，入蛤蜊川熟撈起取出蛤蜊肉，米粉泡軟備用。
2 將蝦米泡軟洗淨切末，香菇亦泡軟切絲備用。
3 鍋熱入油４大匙燒熱，入 **1** 料爆香，續入南瓜、蛤蜊肉拌炒，最後入 **2** 料煮開，再入米粉炒勻即可。

600g.(1⅓lb.) --------- clams　　300g.(10½oz.) -- dried rice
580g.(1¼lb.) --- pumpkins　　noodles (thin)

1
　•12 sections green onion
　•20g.(⅔oz.) dried baby shrimp
　•5g.(⅙oz.) dried black mushrooms

2
　•1C.water
　•1¼t.salt
　•¼t.black pepper

1 Pare pumpkins, discard seeds, and shred. Boil the water in a pot, drop the clams in until they are cooked. Drain and remove the shells. Soak rice noodles in water until softened.
2 Soften shrimp in water, wash and mince. Soften mushrooms in water and shred.
3 Heat the wok, add 4T. oil and heat; stir fry **1** until fragrant, add pumpkins and clams to fry. Add **2** and bring to a boil. Mix in the rice noodles evenly and serve.

味全家政班

味全家政班創立於民國五十年，經過三十餘年的努力，它不只是國內歷史最悠久的家政研習班，更成為一所正式學制之外的專門學校。

創立之初，味全家政班以教授中國菜及研習烹飪技術為主，因教學成果良好，備受各界讚譽，乃於民國五十二年，增闢插花、工藝、美容等各門專科，精湛的師資，教學內容的充實，深獲海內外的肯定與好評。

三十餘年來，先後來班參與研習的學員已近二十萬人次，學員的足跡遍及台灣以外，更有許多國外的團體或個人專程抵台，到味全家政班求教，在習得中國菜烹調的精髓後，或返回居住地經營餐飲業，或擔任家政教師，或獲聘為中國餐廳主廚者大有人在，成就倍受激賞。

近年來，味全家政班亞力研究開發改良中國菜餚，並深入國際間，採集各種精緻、道地美食，除了樹立中華文化「食的精神」外，並將各國烹飪口味去蕪存菁，擷取地方特色。為了確保這些研究工作更加落實，我們特將這些集合海內外餐飲界與研發單位的經典之作，以縝密的拍攝技巧與專業編輯，出版各式食譜，以做傳承。

薪傳與發揚中國烹飪的藝術，是味全家政班一貫的理念，日後，也將秉持宗旨，永續不輟。

Wei-Chuan Cooking School

Since its establishment in 1961, Wei-Chuan Cookin School has made a continuous commitment towar improving and modernizing the culinary art of cookin and special skills training. As a result, it is the olde and most successful school of its kind in Taiwan.

In the beginning, Wei-Chuan Cooking School wa primarily teaching and researching Chinese cookin techniques. However, due to popular demand, th curriculum was expanded to cover courese in flowe arrangements, handcrafts, beauty care, dress makin and many other specialized fields by 1963.

The fact that almost 200,000 students, from Taiwa and other countries all over the world, have matric lated in this school can be directly attributed to the hig quality of the teaching staff and the excellent curric lum provided to the studends. Many of the graduate have become successful restaurant owners and chef and in numerous cases, respected teachers.

While Wei-Chuan Cooking School has always bee committed to developing and improving Chinese cu sine, we have recently extended our efforts towar gathering information and researching recipes from defferent provinces of China. With the same dedica tion to accuracy and perfection as always, we hav begun to publish these authentic regional gourm recipes for our devoted readers. These new publica tions will continue to reflect the fine tradition of qualit our public has grown to appreciate and expect.

純青食譜 傳遞溫馨

微波爐第一冊
- 62道菜
- 112頁
- 中英對照
- 平裝250元
  精裝300元

微波爐第二冊
- 76道菜
- 128頁
- 中英對照
- 平裝280元
  精裝330元

健康食譜
- 100道菜
- 120頁
- 中英對照
- 平裝250元

素食
- 84道菜
- 116頁
- 中英對照
- 平裝250元
  精裝300元

台灣菜
- 73道菜
- 120頁
- 中英對照
- 平裝280元
  精裝330元

四川菜
- 115道菜
- 96頁
- 中英對照
- 平裝280元

飲茶食譜
- 88道菜
- 128頁
- 中英對照
- 平裝300元
  精裝350元

家常100
- 100道菜
- 96頁
- 中英對照
- 平裝250元

嬰幼兒食譜
- 140道菜
- 104頁
- 中文版
- 平裝250元

麵食精華篇
- 87道菜
- 96頁
- 中英對照
- 平裝250元

麵食家常篇
- 91道菜
- 96頁
- 中英對照
- 平裝250元

米食傳統篇
- 82道菜
- 96頁
- 中英對照
- 平裝250元

 純青出版社
台北市松江路125號5樓
TEL：(02)5074902・5084331
劃撥帳號：12106299

純青食譜　版權所有

局版台業字第3884號
中華民國83年6月初版發行
定價：新台幣貳佰伍拾元整